Becoming Healthy, Staying Healthy

Heart Advice from an Acupuncturist

Becoming Healthy, Staying Healthy

Heart Advice from an Acupuncturist

ANN CECIL-STERMAN

W PRESS

First edition

Disclaimer and Note: The information presented in this book relates to the subject of what is known as "Traditional Chinese Medicine" and "Classical Chinese Medicine" and is intended solely for use by Licensed Acupuncturists and students under the supervised study of acupuncture through an accredited educational institution. The information in this work is not to be used or acted upon by an unlicensed, untrained, or unsupervised individual. The Author and Publisher do not advocate or endorse self-diagnosis, self-medication, or treatment by unlicensed individuals under any circumstances. Chinese Medicine is a regulated profession and subject to the jurisdiction of the individual states as well as local and national professional and accrediting organizations. Individuals are strongly encouraged to perform their own due diligence and seek guidance and referrals from these organizations or other licensed professionals.

This book contains many fine points developed through many years of clinical practice. May this book serve all those who practice and receive the precious gift of Chinese Medicine.

Cover design, book design, and diagrams by Cody Dodo
Photographs including cover photograph by Ravi Zohar Sterman

ISBN: 978-1-954773-05-9

To Miriam

Contents

Author's Note

Having the knowledge to cultivate one's own health on a daily basis is the key to a life of greater freedom. Not only does daily care enhance the quality of one's life in general, it keeps the body prepared to deal with the inevitable challenges we can face any day: adverse weather, pathogenic factors, poor quality or spoiled food, exposure to chemicals, emotional trauma, accidents, overwork, stress. The various chapters of life—from infancy through the natural process of aging—need not be fraught with difficulties and diminishing vibrancy. In this book you will find suggestions that help the body relax, heal, and stay tuned. A healthy body yields a vastly freer life: one of increased mobility, less pain, greater clarity of vision, senses and mind, freedom in expression and resolution of emotions, more room for happiness, and more lightness of being. I have been dispensing this golden advice in my acupuncture clinic and to students all over the world for over twenty years following and during my deep training in Classical Chinese medicine with Jeffrey Yuen. Countless people can attest to its life-changing effects. May you, too, find a deeper connection to your innate capacity, and encounter the increased quality of health you are hoping for, or haven't yet imagined.

1. Tune to the Season and to Time

We've built our lives often far from our warm, subtropical origins. We invented electric lights to stay awake in the dark, and heavy curtains to stay asleep past dawn. We heat our homes in winter and cool them in summer. As modern as we are, deep within we are still following natural seasonal rhythms. Comfort is important, but if we overcool or overheat our living spaces, the body is not able to adjust to the current season, or to the time of day. The body is obstructed from going through its natural cycles of storing fat for winter, or generating excitement for spring, for example. If we over-illuminate our living space at night, we limit the hormonal shifts the body needs to make as the sun goes down. This makes it difficult to fall into a deep sleep easily and with consistency.

During the winter, our bodies go into conservation mode. In Chinese medicine, this is shown in the pulses as they sink noticeably deeper in the wrist—the body is conserving energy for spring and summer. Being quiet at night in winter will honor this natural process and enable you to feel more harmonious. During the evenings, go with the season and practice enjoying the substantially slower pace that winter invites, rather than trying to duplicate the excitement of summer and then feeling disappointed. To ensure hormonal changes occur in balance, minimize the ambient light in your home and make sure that there is at least one dark corner in the room. This signals to the body that the sun has set and that we should prepare for rest. Sleep in turn deepens, and the regulation of digestion, hormones, and mental function is maximized.

Bright lights late in the day during winter, especially when combined with over-heated living spaces, cause the body to think it's summer, and that it must store fuel (fat) for the winter. If your lights are bright in the winter, you will eat more than you need, gain extra weight, and generally not feel well.

In spring and summer it is desirable to go to bed later and to get up earlier as we naturally open up more energy; the days are longer, food is fresh and ready for harvest, and it's beautiful to be out in the sun.

2. Awaken Gently

If you need an alarm in the morning, avoid loud sounds. Consider using one of those clocks with a beep that starts softly and gradually gets louder until you can hear it. The manner in which you wake is important. Waking up to a shocking noise instantly puts you in a defensive mode, affecting your state throughout the day.

You might be one of those lucky people who can decide on a waking time and simply open your eyes at that time. I've met many people who can do this, and my parents could do it to the minute just by deciding on the time the night before. Perhaps this was because they grew up with no alarm clocks. It's worth a try to wake up into more peace.

3. Move Your Bowels. Warm Morning Water

Drink a glass of warm water every morning when you wake up. Normally, first thing in the morning, the stomach is empty. A glass of plain, flat, warm water taken upon waking will go straight through your digestive tract to your large intestine. The large intestine takes all the water it needs to moisten your stool, allowing your bowels to move easily before breakfast. It can take a couple of weeks for your body to get the hang of it, and soon it can become routine.

The ancient masters said that for good health, when the large intestine is full, the stomach should be empty, and when the stomach is full, the large intestine should be empty. If this is not the case, an energetic standoff ensues, and the digestive tract gets sluggish. Encouraging your bowels to move with a glass of warm water on waking, or at least well before breakfast, and then having a bowel movement before breakfast, leaves the stomach free to properly welcome your breakfast and pass it through to the intestines. The stomach is not so enthusiastic about moving food through when it knows that there is a roadblock ahead. The practice of "warm morning water" is also freeing for the mind, as the feeling of digestive freedom in turn supports a willingness to move forward in any endeavor.

A Push against History

Many people report that they don't have bowel movements in the morning. Others don't remember their bowels moving every day at all. If you don't have regular morning movements, even if it has been a life-long habit, try the following exercise. This simple practice often brings excellent results along with a feeling of great freedom.

1. On waking, drink a glass of warm water—large if possible. The water must be quite warm.
2. If you can, squat down with your feet wide apart and your bottom close to the floor. Put your palms together. Rest your elbows on the inside surface of your knees. Stay there as long as you're comfortable.
3. Eat as many figs (dried or fresh) as you feel like.
4. Squat again. (Repeat step 2.)
5. While in the squat position, if you can, rotate from side to side like an oscillating fan, several times.

The combination of warm water followed by the hundreds of seeds in the figs will move the large intestine, freeing up space in the tract for your breakfast when it's time. The figs, even while in the mouth, send a message to the large intestine to move. Once your bowels are regulated, stop this practice. The body can become habituated to any measure that is repeated long term, and we don't want the effectiveness of this method to be weakened through overuse.

4. Liberation Style Hydration

Drink liquids at room temperature, or better still, warm. The digestive tract moves freely when its natural temperature is complemented with warmth. If the digestive tract is cooled, its motion slows, sometimes so much so that the abdomen tightens and cramps. In response, the body gathers qi to try to prompt movement. When cold overwhelms that gathered qi, the combination of cold and qi becomes stuck, creating frequent and sharp cramping.

Usually, lab tests will initially show nothing because the pathogenic factor (stagnated qi and cold) is not measurable. Over time, as the accumulation of qi continues, and since qi is naturally warm, heat builds up in the gut, resulting in inflammation. At that point, tests will show irritation or even damage to the lining of the gut. We might then think that cooling off the inflammation with cold and raw food and beverages is wise, and we might even crave cold water and drinks, but this will further aggravate and prolong the inflammation because cold slows, contracts, and suppresses, trapping the original cold and the resulting inflammation with it. Drinking your water (or beverage) warm and keeping everything that you consume warm or very warm is the single easiest way to alleviate this kind of pain because warmth actively moves qi, and moving qi releases pain.

5. News Diet

Try to avoid news at night or in the morning. If you wake up and engage in news or media right away, your stress level will be elevated before your day has even begun, taxing your liver and setting the scene for various mental and physical tensions. This is because after hearing bad news, the body tightens in defense. The qi that runs through the liver must then battle to relax the musculature again. This creates stress in the liver itself. The liver has key branches on its energy pathways that go to the eyes and the brain. Constant stress eventually harms the eyes and brain, causing visual disturbances, or visual tiredness, and ultimately, irregularities in brain function.

Looking at the news in the evening can complicate things further, because with every heartbeat, the liver is unable to receive its nightly increase in blood flow. Without that increase, deep sleep is elusive.

All these things in play, a person will have a constant feeling of never being fully settled. They may even consider that normal. Shifting the news habit will help this tremendously. The best time for news is in the afternoon, where there's a big buffer between the two crucial feel-good times.

6. Break Fast

Eat some breakfast soon after you get up in the morning. The qi running through your pancreas and spleen is responsible for your general feeling of vitality, your clarity of thought, the movement of your limbs, and the distribution of nutrients and warmth. Both organs are awakened by action in the digestive tract. Eating a good breakfast in the morning will maximize your energy and clarity of thought for the whole day.

Fasting

When new patients arrive for their morning appointment with weak spleen and pancreas pulses and a slightly racing kidney/adrenaline pulse, I often ask whether they are fasting. As a rule, as much as possible, one's qi should be derived from post-natal qi. That means that it should come from the food you ate that day. If you fast, especially if you skip breakfast, your body must reach for prenatal qi, the precious kidney yang and yin that you were born with. The activation of adrenaline is stimulating, giving the feeling that fasting is invigorating, but this is false and expensive energy. This deep pre-natal qi is of limited supply. If you're not hungry, just eat a very small amount of grain. It may take several days or weeks but it will kick-start your appetite as the body learns to undo its habit of activating kidney yang to get you going. If you are worried about "detoxing" remember that every cell in your body is detoxing every second. Try not to introduce toxins in the first place, and your body will catch up.

What's a good breakfast? A gluten, dairy and sugar-free one. And wet breakfasts are supreme. Some protein is important, since it is warming and moving, in alignment with the spirit of morning. Make any of the many non-glutenous grains into a porridge that you might start soaking the night before to save time. Or if you have time, pancakes or waffles with the same non-glutenous flour, with cooked berries on the side, and an egg. Or an omelette. Or leftover dinner warmed up. Or a soup.

If you have no appetite in the morning or if you get nauseous with morning eating, your stomach qi is misdirected and not descending properly. You might try carrot soup.

7. Wet Hair Hassles

Dry your hair after you wash it. Wet, cold hair cools down the back of the neck, leaving you prey to the common cold. Catching a cold is a surprisingly easy way to invite physical havoc.

If you really don't have time to dry your hair, make sure it is fully off your neck and then cover the entire area with a scarf and hat so that the wind gates (the vulnerable areas at the back of your neck) are warm and protected.

Sometimes if I find that a person has contracted a cold because they went out with wet hair, they'll say, "My grandmother used to tell me that I would catch a cold that way but I figured it's just an old wives' tale". That precious generation is now long gone and greatly missed; they were indeed wise and they knew many important things that cannot be measured.

8. Scarf Rescue

Put a scarf around your neck if you're going out in a breeze or wind. It may seem odd, but wearing a scarf in windy conditions is one of the most fundamental ways you can prevent a decline in your health. The common cold—we call it wind-cold in Chinese medicine—is a bringer of change. It comes in to upgrade something, like a tiny software tweak. It can come and go in a single breath without us knowing. Or, the body might respond with a quick succession of sneezes and their accompanying micro-sweats to expel the cold along with something that doesn't belong (substance, perhaps phlegm, or even thoughts). Then we return to the day, recalibrated in an almost imperceptible way.

Sometimes a common cold can become a major event; it can slow us down as it takes a while to engage the body in a bigger change before resolving. These colds often cause the body to create a fever to burn up something that we've been harboring for a long time. The pathogenic factors and their passage are not measurable, making the invitation to change ever mysterious.

The wind gates—entry and exit sites for the common cold—are at the back of the neck. If this area is bare and there is wind or cold, the gates are vulnerable to stronger invasion, especially if we are tired or not well-nourished. The cold enters and the region tightens to limit more entry. The body then goes into overdrive to defend against the invasion of more cold through the back of the neck, bringing what we call defensive qi (wei qi) to the area, tightening the neck further, and raising the shoulders—creating a protective stance. The only way to get the trapped cold to exit is to seek shelter and warm up, perhaps even to the point of inducing a sweat to facilitate the exit of the cold. If you feel a cold coming on, move it out straightaway.

To push out a cold, your body needs three things:

- warmth to counter the cold

• fluids to create a sweat, and
• strength to create the movement of warmth and fluids.

In other words, rest and hydrate. The old ways of resting while someone brings you hot soup as you recover are based on that central tenet. Nobody likes the inconvenience of having a cold: the stiff neck, the headache, the runny nose, the sneezing. These are all ways the body pushes the cold out, and that process takes a little time. The fatigue is the body's urge to rest.

In our modern life, we just try to keep going, often medicating to suppress the runny nose and to push through fatigue. We try to force ourselves to maintain normal activity, either due to refusal to yield to healing time, or the sheer necessity to work. If you cannot rest properly by stopping work for a while, drink plenty of warm water (or better still, hot soup), and see if your body can be persuaded to push it out. Take a very warm bath or shower, put all your clothes on, jump under a heavy pile of blankets, and allow yourself to sweat for one minute. This can open your pores and release the "cold" from your body. We want to resolve it by pushing it out, not suppressing it. Taking a drug or a cold remedy might alleviate your symptoms, but it does so by suppressing them, sending the cold deeper in the body and therefore making it less apparent to the senses and easier to ignore. Properly applied herbal treatments don't suppress symptoms but nourish fluids to help push the cold out. Conserve your energy so that your body can gather qi to create a fever and sweat.

If expulsion of the cold doesn't happen, it takes up residence and the body must find other ways to contain it, to keep it away from the internal arena including the organs, themselves. (By the way, the journey of cold through the body is the subject of one of the greatest Chinese medicine texts, Treatise of Cold Diseases.) Classical Chinese wisdom holds that the common cold is the beginning of "a thousand diseases". What seems like a minor annoyance is treated seriously in Chinese medical theory. Progressions of cold-induced illnesses ranging from mild to severe arthritis or other chronic degenerative diseases that occur when the body cannot push cold out are described in the classical texts as numerous and serious.

Once the cold is trapped, the body—in its quest to keep the disruption away from the viscera (the organs)—puts the cold away in the joints where it can stay quiet. So the old adage that cold affects your bones and causes arthritis can be quite true. If the body doesn't have the resources to keep it quiet in the joints, the cold—along with the defensive qi that brought it there—leaks out and goes rogue. It then affects the joint itself, and can become more internal, ultimately creating many problems.

Better to avoid the cold in the first place. In order to keep the neck warm enough for defense and for eradication of cold, and to keep the body from being invaded by cold in the first place, it is essential to wear a scarf, or high-necked clothing when outside in cool weather, a breeze, or wind.

Drafts and breezes can crop up anywhere. The most common encounters are outside when a sudden cold breeze catches you off guard. Airplanes, trains, and buses can be a special problem, especially those that don't allow you to control the wind coming down on your head. Also common is the experience of being overheated in the summer and walking into in air-conditioned places, where the body is shocked not only by the change in temperature, but by the unseasonal nature of the temperature. All these incidents can be much less damaging if you can reach into your bag or pocket and pull out scarf—even a thin one.

Some acupuncturists are so concerned about people taking drugs for the common cold that they offer a quick common cold treatment at less than their usual fee. Acupuncturists help ensure it doesn't progress by treating what we call the sinew channels. The simplest of these treatments involves two needles: one at your pinky finger and one at your pinky toe. You can easily mimic this treatment: drink some warm water and then firmly and frequently pinch the points shown below without hurting the skin.

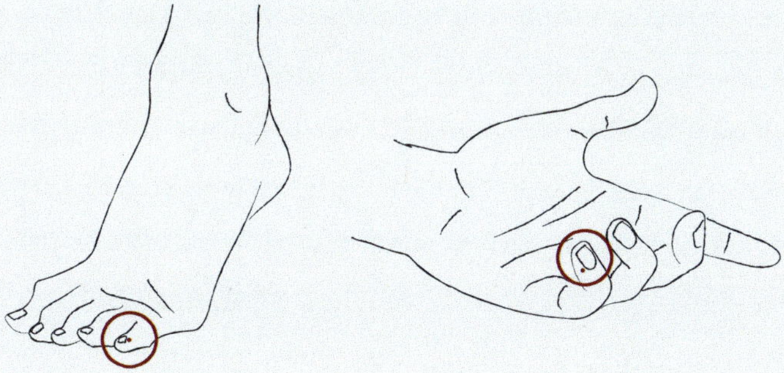

9. Blessed Sneezes

It's impolite to sneeze right in front of someone—that's something we learn early in life. Then we see people stifle sneezes, even when alone or outdoors, and this isn't good either!

Sneezing is a critically important mechanism that enables the body to expel pathogenic factors (especially cold) before they have a chance to enter deeply into the respiratory system. Let sneezes happen. Let the nose and mouth be open and free during the sneeze, even if you're sneezing into a tissue or an elbow. The pathogenic factor must exit and not be stifled. If you can't stop sneezing, that's a different matter. Remove the cause of the irritation. Are you reacting to flowers nearby? Did you just buy a piece of furniture that's letting off noxious gasses? Do you have wall-to-wall carpet, which is a breeding ground for dust mites? Is your pillow disintegrating? Did you eat something cold, raw, dairy-based, full of sugar, or glutinous? Is someone around you wearing perfumed body lotion, shampoos or chemical deodorants? Is your laundry detergent toxic, laden with perfumes, dyes and poured from a brightly colored bottle? If everything seems threatening and you feel constantly under attack, look hard at everything around you and make major changes. Taking allergy medications might stop sneezing and eyes watering, but in doing so they prevent the body sounding the alarm (sneeze) and eliminating toxins, leaving you vulnerable to deeper problems later.

See more about this kind of sensitivity on page 58.

10. Low Back Wrap

Keep your lower back warm and enjoy the resulting increase in your energy levels. The energy flowing through your kidneys and lower back is like a power plant responsible for generating all the energy your body needs to perform its functions. If these areas are cold, they spend stored energy trying to warm themselves, depleting your total energy level. Also, if the kidneys and lower back are cold, yang qi that is generated in that region cannot move freely to other parts of your body, causing you to become less flexible and less efficient. Cold in the lower back contributes significantly to a great number of problems including incontinence, back issues, cold hands and feet, varicose veins, depression, infertility, hemorrhoids, stiffness, pain, allergies, and early aging. Dress to cover your kidneys well—they're higher in your back than you think—and avoid cold foods and drinks. If you're aware of cold in your back, your internal cold is advanced. Wrap a scarf around your midsection and waist under your clothes. Eliminate your cold habits and apply a hot pad to your back whenever you are seated until the cold has broken up. Your energy levels will improve dramatically.

11. Sparkling Fizzles

Stay hydrated by drinking flat water rather than sparkling water, soda, or anything carbonated. Mass-produced carbonated beverages begin as plain flat water with flavorings. The fluid is placed in a pressurized tank and carbon dioxide is then forced into it. The result is that the water which is naturally yin (very quiet with a downward directionality) becomes very yang (excited and moving). Carbonated beverages are understood by

the body to be a moving force, not the hydrating fluids we might think they are. The body reacts by trying to excrete them quickly, often using its fluids to usher out the invasion. The result is that carbonated beverages have a net dehydrating effect. Clean, plain, flat water hydrates, though. And so does fat, but more on that later.

12. Food Focus

When you eat—just eat! Eating is a process involving looking, smelling, touching, and tasting. Our digestive tract specifically prepares for the foods we encounter as we see, smell, taste, and chew our food. This fine-tunes the digestive process in countless ways. The pancreas and spleen—whose energetics are responsible for transforming your food into useful substances—can become stressed if you're watching a movie or the news, or arguing with the person across the table. Digestion is then incomplete, adding more stress to the gut. Dysfunction of the qi of digestion is the primary cause of excess body weight, weak limbs, coldness, puffiness, swellings, blurred vision, obsessive thought, and fatigue.

13. Food Blessings

Bless your food. Call it what you will; hold your hands together to help focus, then bless your food, give thanks for it, become aware of where it's from and how you are going to eat it. Just the simple act of consciously being grateful for your food alters the way your body receives it. It maximizes the healing and nourishing nature of the food. This is a practice in all religions, and it's a practice that can benefit everyone.

If you can't think up a blessing without it feeling weird, just close your eyes and say, "Thanks for this food." Once you get into the habit of blessing your food, you'll find that the practice of gratitude creates an avalanche of tiny shifts in the way you view the world. Over time, the world will feel softer and less aggressive because you'll find yourself focusing on other things to be grateful for.

If you're looking for food blessing ideas, here are a few to get you started until you come up with much better ones: "I'm so grateful for this food." If you're eating away from home: "I'm grateful for this food, and grateful to the people who grew, tended, transported and prepared it for me/us." And more: "I am grateful for the nourishment this food brings my body." "I'm grateful for each grain of rice, each bean, each leaf, and the life force given me by this animal."

14. Grazing Pace

Eat more slowly. In Chinese medicine the taste of a food has a direct impact on the qi of specific organs. If you really crunch on and taste that sesame seed on your lunch, the energetics of the kidneys are far more nourished than if you swallow without noticing. Tuning your awareness of all aspects of your food has a poignant effect on your body's reception of food.

15. Gut Pain Blues Remedy

Eat cooked food. Easy on the raw. Enjoy more digestive comfort. Digestion thrives in a warm gut and really doesn't do well in a cool one, since cold constricts the natural motility of the gut. This is why you can cramp after ice cream or cold drinks. Raw foods also cool down your digestive system, forcing it to work hard to heat itself up again. Salads are naturally cooling and there are some benefits and certainly pleasures in having them during hot weather. Foods such as lettuce, tomato, and cucumber grow naturally only in the summer and cool the body with their high water content and intrinsic energetic signatures. During winter, when the body needs to stay warm, eating salads introduces an unwelcome cold that impedes digestion. If the gut is cool, it can't "cook" your food. Food must be heated before it can be broken down, and that's so much easier if it arrives in the digestive tract already nicely cooked and warm.

A great irony is that cold and raw food can make you feel terrific in the short term. This is because the body responds to cold by activating a tremendous amount of energy to warm up the gut. This process—though it brings with it a feeling of stimulation and vitality in the short term—steadily depletes the good feeling. Eventually, the ready capacity to spend this qi wanes, and people become exhausted and cold in the long term, especially as they insist on eating salads in winter making themselves even colder.

Raw foodists are among the least healthy people I've seen. They can have loose stools, undigested food in the stool, cold hands and feet, are unable to handle cold weather, they bruise easily, can be foggy headed and anemic, and have trouble becoming pregnant. They often have hemorrhoids, hormonal issues, and all the while try to convince you that they are getting much more nutrition than a person eating cooked food. They have a point: if you give a lab technician some kale for analysis, they'll report that it has more nutrients when raw than after cooking. The raw nature of the food weakens the digestive process since digestion has to work so much harder to break it down. After a while the gut is so weakened that many of those nutrients are not being released sufficiently for absorption anyway. Good cooked food might have fewer nutrients as measured in the lab, but it is inherently strengthening for the gut, leading to consistent access to the nutrients in food. The net effect of eating cooked food is greater nutritional absorption.

16. Home Cooking

Most of your food should be home-cooked. Even if you're simply making a quick omelet in the morning and throwing a few thawed frozen peas in it, do eat at least one home-cooked meal a day. That way, you know exactly what's in your food and you can control its quality and freshness. Good quality food is much more economical when had at home. You're also honoring yourself with the action of feeding yourself. Eventually this whole process can become deeply satisfying. Invest in a thermos and pack a hot lunch of dinner leftovers from the night before. (Put the leftovers in a pan with a splash of water to create steam, put the lid on, and wait until it's hot. It really doesn't take long at all.) A good thermos keeps food hot easily until lunchtime.

If you don't know where to start with cooking your own food, consider my husband's books, *Welcoming Food*, volumes 1 & 2, written just for this purpose. They're quite wonderful, and many people tell us that they are now utterly transformed and kitchen-rescued.

17. Dairy Duty

Reduce dairy intake. According to the great masters, dairy foods are very "damp". That means they sit heavily in the body, are slow to digest, create lots of waste trapping mucus, and add weight to your body. All of those things severely sap your energy as your body tries to rectify the imbalance. In ancient Chinese medicine, dairy foods, rather than being considered actual foods for humans, were considered medicine, because they are so sedating. Dairy as medicine treats stress and mania, along with chronic malnutrition such as being dangerously underweight. Butter is not included in this category because with the milk solids removed, it is very easy to digest—a fat that our bodies intuitively know how to assimilate without raising inflammation.

If you're concerned about not getting enough calcium, eat your choice of dark leafy green vegetables, sesame seeds, lentils, sardines, and seafood. There's much more digestible calcium in those foods than in dairy foods.

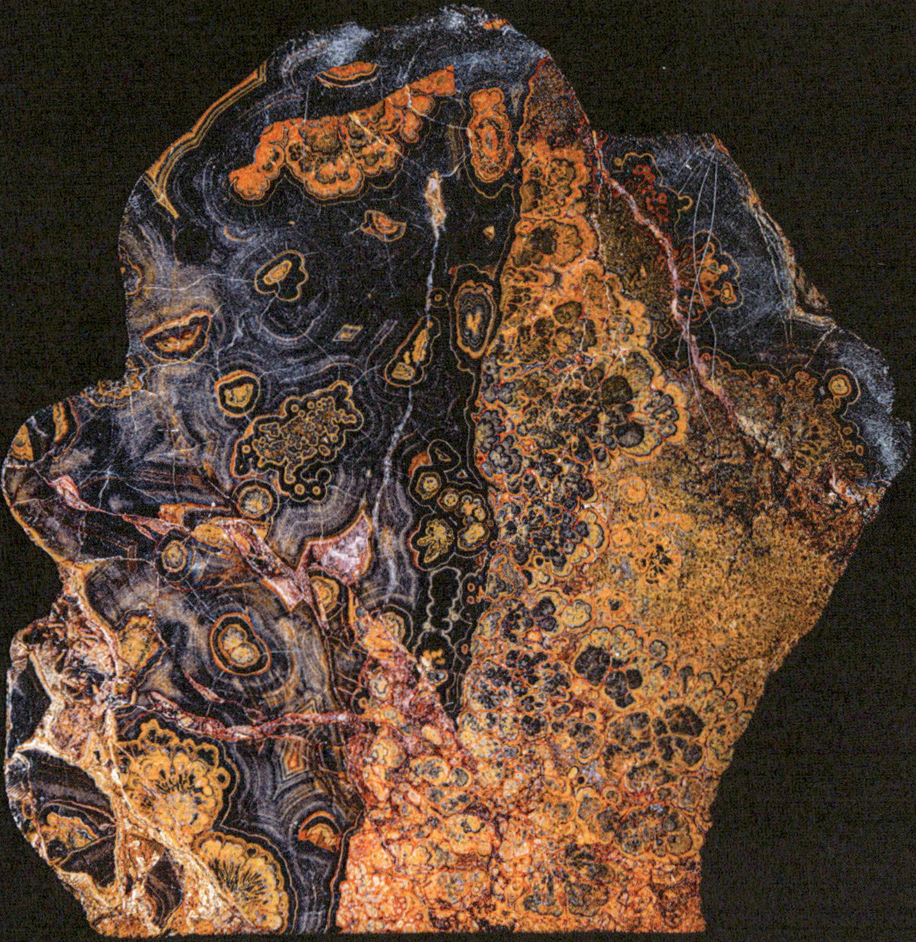

If you love dairy, eat room temperature yogurt, kefir or labneh. These are fermented and already significantly predigested. You'll know if you're eating too much because phlegm will begin to accumulate in your throat or sinuses; you'll be clearing your throat or wishing you could blow your nose, or you may be waking up with crusty eyes. You might be interested in the Harvard University Nurses' Study, a thirty year-long project that unequivocally confirmed what the ancient Chinese had known all along: dairy foods reduce bone density.

18. Chewing It Over

Chew very well. Chewing food well is one of the simplest ways to improve health. Digestion begins in the mouth, with the enzymatic action of saliva already starting the process of breaking down the food. Saliva needs to coat everything that is not protein, and that takes about as long as it does to chew your food into a good mush. A bonus is that when food is in your mouth that long, you can better register its taste. The sense of taste activates the channel of energy that runs through the stomach. These factors enhance the messaging to the digestive tract, fine-tuning the sequential release of acids and hormones, leading to more complete digestion, tailored exactly to that particular combination of foods.

My mother was raised to chew thirty-two times before swallowing and sometimes my grandmother would count them!

19. Lipid Lucidity

Don't be afraid of fat. Be afraid of sugar. All body functions are regulated by hormones, and cholesterol is a hormone building block. If your cholesterol levels are low, you cannot enjoy normal bodily function. Low cholesterol levels are proven indicators for depression, violent behavior, stroke, cancer, and even suicide. You might be interested in the remarkable Framingham Heart study, begun in 1948 and continuing today, that has yet to show a strong correlation between fat intake and heart disease.

When we eat sugar, if we don't use it immediately for energy, the body must store it or it will create inflammatory havoc in the bloodstream. Therefore it's converted into fat, a relatively inert energy storage vehicle. This is not good fat: fat derived from sugar is junk-fat.

Repeated sugar digestion puts tremendous taxation on the spleen, pancreas, and liver, resulting in inflammation of the arteries and, later, the heart. The liver is forced to manufacture cholesterol and then distribute it to the blood vessel walls to soothe and protect them from the threatening inflammation. As sugar consumption becomes habit, the constant irritation of the arterial walls combined with the constant depositing of cholesterol in the walls to rescue them creates cardiovascular disease. Ultimately the arteries can become blocked, causing heart attacks and strokes.

Cholesterol accumulating in the arteries didn't get there due to cholesterol intake; it got there as an intentional ingenious response to sugar intake. To protect your cardiovascular health, remove sugar entirely, except perhaps for special celebrations.

In the United States, sugar is added to about 80 percent of all grocery items. We are trained by manufacturers to believe that bread, yogurt, crackers, soup, cereals, etc., should be sweet, but they are not. Now, so many items are sweetened that many people can't even detect sugar in foods; it's a constant background taste. Since the sugar escalation began, the incidence of heart disease has exploded to become the number one cause of death, while during the same period meat and saturated fat intake has not increased.

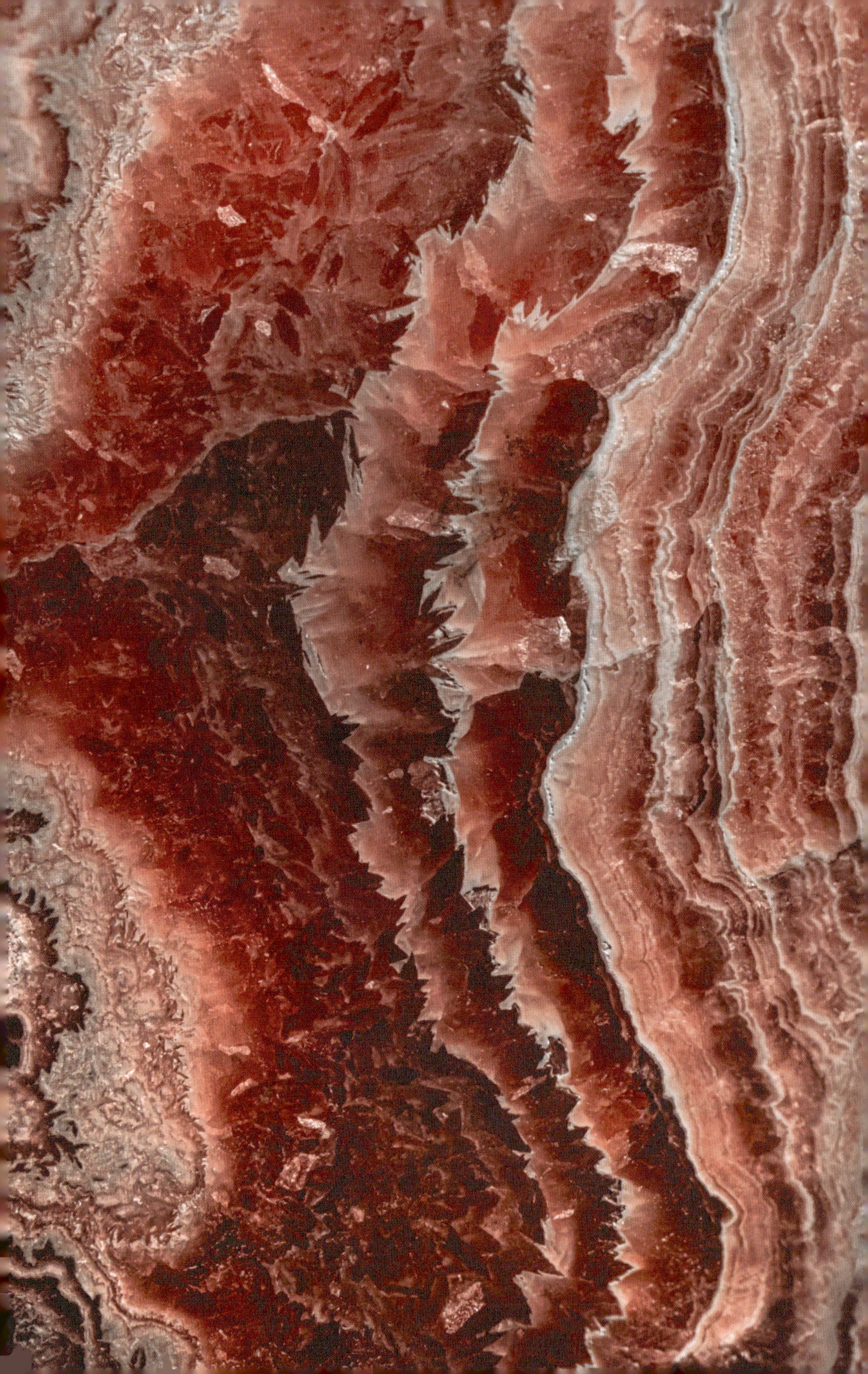

20. Food of Better Comfort

Improve your comfort food. When you are stressed, do you reach for chocolate, cookies, cake, candy, chips, processed foods, and other comforters? These also introduce stress to the body, creating a feeling that we need more comfort, often from these same foods. It's a cycle. Consider changing your comfort foods by switching to things you make yourself. Make your own oatmeal and honey cookies, your own chips from kale or sweet potato, your own gluten-free cake. This eliminates all the additives, staleness, allergens, and the processing in familiar snack foods. Also, the act of making your own snack food can be inherently comforting, calming, and therapeutic.

If you want to take your comfort food in a different direction, try the great old-fashioned comfort food—chicken soup. The smell of soup simmering on the stove has a profoundly comforting effect.

21. Livid Liver

Keep your liver as relaxed as possible by raising the bar on your food choices. In our society we do many things that contribute to tension in the liver, reducing its capacity to store blood and distribute qi. Chief of these is the consumption of coffee, chocolate, and sugar. Eliminating these three things from the diet can dramatically change the way you feel, see, and think. When the liver is relaxed, it is better able to store blood, and therefore to generate qi. That qi forms pathways to the heart, brain, and eyes. If the liver is relaxed, heart functions become smoother, the eyes relax, vision improves, and the brain is better nourished, calming everything.

As you decide to give these three things up, do it gradually. Reduce the quantity slowly and steadily to avoid the terrible headaches of caffeine withdrawal. It takes at least two weeks to complete the process. You'll likely feel much more relaxed and sleep much more deeply.

22. Eye Rest

Rest your eyes. In today's world so much of our work and relaxation time has us sitting in front of computer or television screens. Some of my patients say that by the end of the day their eyes sting, ache, or feel tired from focusing at exactly the same distance for hours on end. This is eye taxation.

Taxing your eyes can lead to headaches, fatigue, grumpiness, and tight muscles, particularly the neck muscles. In our current culture, many of us strain our eyes

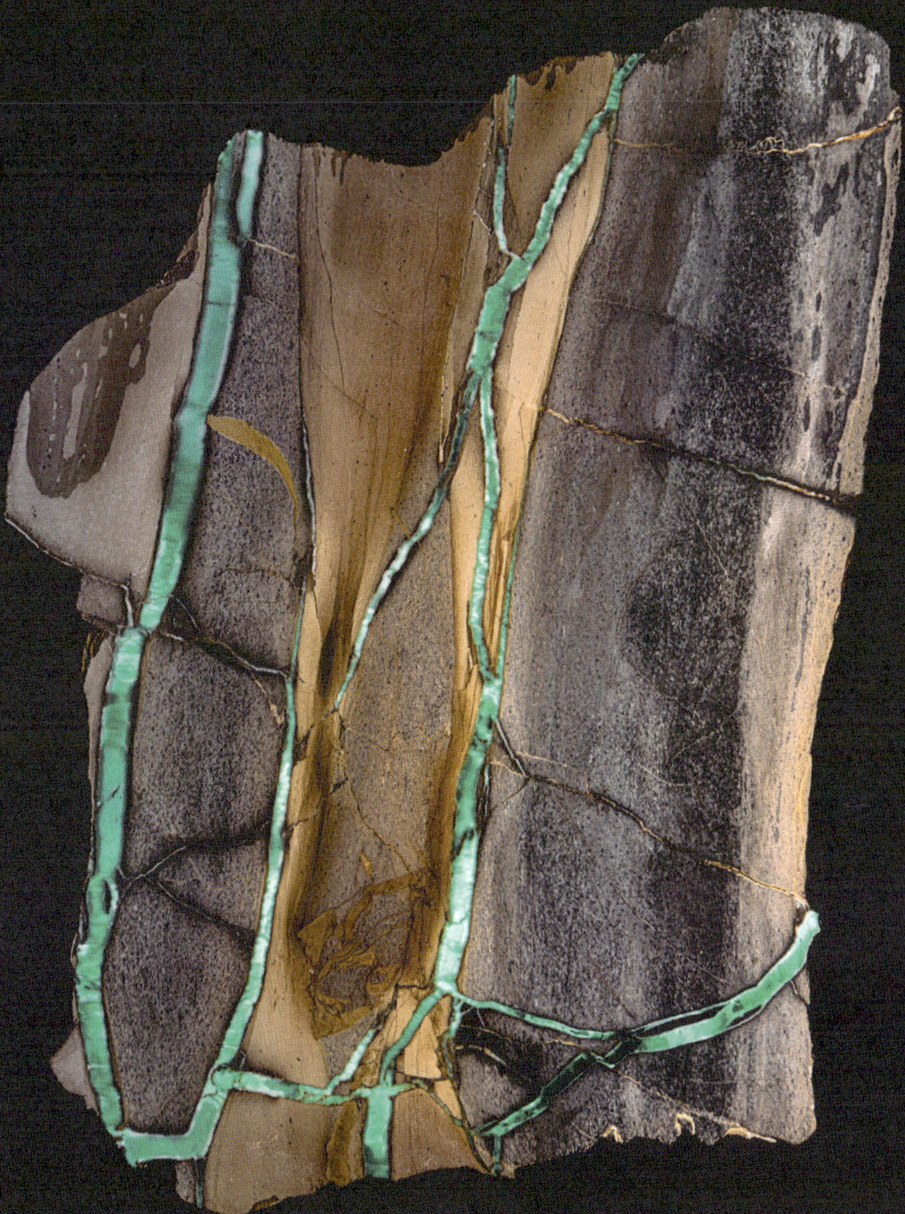

every day for long periods. If you work with concentrated eye focus, take breaks every hour. If you work at a computer, take as many breaks from your screen as you can. Even just looking up and focusing on something far away for a few seconds provides crucial relief for our visual focus.

When you are at your computer, turn the light down on your screen as far as you can to soften the light on your eyes. When you're talking on the phone, turn your computer screen to dark, rather than look at the screen as you're on the phone. Take genuine lunch breaks, away from electronics. And wear blue light glasses to filter out the harsh blue light that assaults the eyes.

Working at a screen all day is immensely tiring because communication between people is designed to be eye to eye and heart to heart, and in the same physical space. Direct in-person communication allows a warm circulation of qi from the heart of one person to the heart of the other. Because this communication is the hallmark of humanity, and because humanity exists to experience an expansive love, in-person exchange is inherently energizing. People (often unknowingly) work extra hard to make a connection happen through a screen and this effort further depletes energy. The result is that even people on a harmonious team working and talking remotely with one another will always feel there is something missing in the communication. You could call that something the element of humanity. When possible, get together.

23. Uterus Unrest

The uterus must be kept warm. Countless times women have come into the office presenting with severe period pain. Nearly always, they are actually cold to the touch on the abdomen below the navel. (I'm wondering whether at this point you, dear reader, are tired of hearing about cold, but it is the cause of so much misery and I want this to be an absolutely clear message.) If the belly is cold to the touch, there will be difficulty moving blood in that region. The qi that moves blood from the liver to the uterus stagnates from the cold, causing tension that creates pain. The situation is worsened in states of dehydration or low blood volume.

The teenage habit of baring the midriff in any weather is a recipe for period pain and later, even for difficulty in conceiving. As the cold becomes advanced, menstrual periods can dramatically lengthen as qi weakens and fails systemically to contain blood. In cases where there is a tendency to under-eat or where there is lack of nourishment, periods can even dramatically shorten as blood production is weak. Menstrual health depends upon the availability of sufficient blood and qi. The contributions of qi from the digestive tract, liver, and lungs must be warm for the shifts in the cycle to be smooth. Individual problems can arise according to the particular ways an individual's body responds to cold, poor digestion, and relative deficiency of blood.

To keep the uterus warm, keep it covered. The lower belly should feel warm at all times, both internally and to the touch. For that to happen, warm food, warm water, and warm clothing are the ticket.

Years ago two college roommates who were best friends at music school came to the office complaining of very long periods. The periods were about twenty days long for both women. (It's a common phenomenon that periods often become synchronized among friends, but I hadn't seen menstrual pathology in sync before.) The two women were exhausted, overly slim, and very pale. When I took their wrist pulses, I found similar results: they were very tight, especially in the positions of the middle and lower regions of the abdomen. I was able to guess almost immediately that they both were eating a lot of sushi, perhaps every day, and that in both women this was creating an enormous amount of cold in the digestive tract, which then descended to the lower abdomen, where it was affecting the uterus. They looked at me in utter astonishment. Yes, it was every day and they loved their sushi. On the table, their lower abdomens were each very cold to the touch. We had a long discussion about raw and cold foods, stressing that sushi, while spectacular food, is a luxury, meant to be eaten in very small quantities, not too often, and always with hot soup and other hot foods. They became convinced that it was a good idea to give it up completely until their periods returned to normal. It took a few weeks until that happened, and then all was smooth sailing, their sushi consumption remained restrained, and they didn't experience that issue again.

24. GMO OMG

Avoid GMOs to stay light in spirit and body. Genetically modified organisms often contain components that are not readily recognized as foods by the gut. They have extra and altered proteins in them which we call "rogue proteins". The body identifies these as foreign entities and mounts an immune response against them. That response creates inflammation in the gut, or, importantly, anywhere in the body where an inflammatory response may already be underway. In turn, the heat of the inflammation cues the body to create mucus or phlegm to quell that heat. These combine to create damp-heat, a kind of phlegm that is deposited in various places in the gut, in the interstitial fluids, and in the joints. This type of weight gain is almost impossible to lose when the consumption of GMOs continues. Many people

are utterly baffled as to why they are gaining so much weight and why they can't drop the weight even if they move to a calorie-restrictive diet still comprising GMO foods. The body will not allow the depletion of the wet mass because it is defending the body against the ravages and erosion of inflammation. The body is acting with its full intelligence: as long as inflaming substances such as GMOs are being consumed, the systemic heavy damp deposits will continue to pile up. As part of a sensible plan to lose weight or reduce inflammation, remove all GMOs and processed foods. Your body will become accustomed to not having to maintain the heavy defense and will begin to clear what is no longer needed.

Let's Talk About Processed Food

Foods come from farms, but not the way they used to. Our markets are increasingly filled with food-based-edibles wrapped in flashy branding: the world of processed foods. And while it is true that "food processing" began with preservation techniques thousands of years ago, food processing has become radically different with modern food chemistry and the explosive growth of packaged product. What is available in supermarkets has shifted so quickly that the term ultra-processed foods is needed to differentiate traditional foods such as pickles, dried apricots, and old-world sausages from the snacks and meats that are popular today—all things designed for shelf-life and advertising appeal rather than wellness or true food satisfaction.

Ultra-processed foods combine NASA-inspired instant meals with complex chemical additives that have been tested for habit-forming appeal—additives for taste, color, and stability. The packaging is also carefully crafted for sales-appeal and often infinite shelf-life. Packaging itself is increasingly seen as a threat to health. The new word obesogen refers to any substance found in food packaging, household cleaning products, or cosmetics that disrupts metabolism, contributes to inflammation or to obesity. These chemicals, dyes and finishes either penetrate the food or penetrate the skin as we touch the packaging.

The food industry would have us believe that it's a short jump from traditional food practices to modern processing. The time-tested ways—some ancient—involve no additional ingredients except perhaps water, salt or spices to taste. They include pickling, drying, salting, freezing, fermenting, and smoking. In the 1800s safe canning was developed. In the early 1900s, frozen food became available. In these methods, the integrity of the food is maintained. Modern processing, also known as ultra-processing, is quite different in that it strips fluids and nutrients and adds chemicals, [often made from food derivatives]. These chemicals, not being food, make digestion difficult, and irritate the gut, which in turn creates inflammation and its sequelae of discomfort and disease.

Resisting enticing marketing and instead shopping nearly entirely in the fresh food sections of your markets is more important than ever before; the difference is significant. It's the difference between health and illness. What you put in your body becomes you. Even foods marketed as wholesome, gluten-free, or organic can be ultra-processed. Food-safety laws and regulations are co-written with industry and can be lax and overly permissive. For best health, whenever possible, have meals that our grandmothers and great-grandmothers would be able to recognize all the way from farm to table.

25. CoffeeChoc Con

Coffee is a problem. Chocolate, too. We hear that coffee offers all kinds of super-healthy nutrients in the overlap of science reporting and feel-good media. Nothing is good for everyone. The people who should have less (or no) coffee are those who tend toward: high blood pressure, tension headaches, indigestion, bowel problems, insomnia or other sleep issues, or a sense of being easily irritated or angered.

Staying hydrated is essential for maintaining a sense of vitality and suppleness, and to maintain the normal, constant clearing of waste from every cell. Hydration depends on two broad principles: the consumption of hydrating beverages and foods, and the elimination from the diet of actively dehydrating foods and beverages. There are three reasons coffee is a strong dehydrator. First, it is the seed of a drupe fruit, like a mango or cherry pit or a peach stone, all of which are used in Chinese herbal medicine to drain excess fluids. Second, coffee is bitter. In Chinese medicine dietetic understanding, each taste has directionality. The bitter taste has a downward vector, pointing toward the kidneys and bladder, stimulating them to pass fluids. Third, coffee is concentrated; it takes a lot of beans to make a single cup. The human body is geared to treat concentrates as something to clear, since most poisons in nature are bitter and concentrated. The liver reacts, since it's responsible for the processing and eradication of toxins. It drops into the bloodstream some of the toxic load it was holding so that it has room to deal with the incoming threat.

Then the liver turns its attention to the incoming toxin (the coffee). It is stimulated to flush the toxins out, allowing them to exit through the hepatic portal vein, which connects to the kidneys. When the kidneys sense that the blood is becoming overloaded with something concentrated (i.e. toxic), the adrenal glands kick in, preparing the body to eradicate the toxins quickly by raising the heart rate, in turn creating cardiovascular stress. This is "the caffeine high." It's a completely fake, artificial high. It causes the expenditure of bodily fluids and energy, resulting in dryness even in the body's interior.

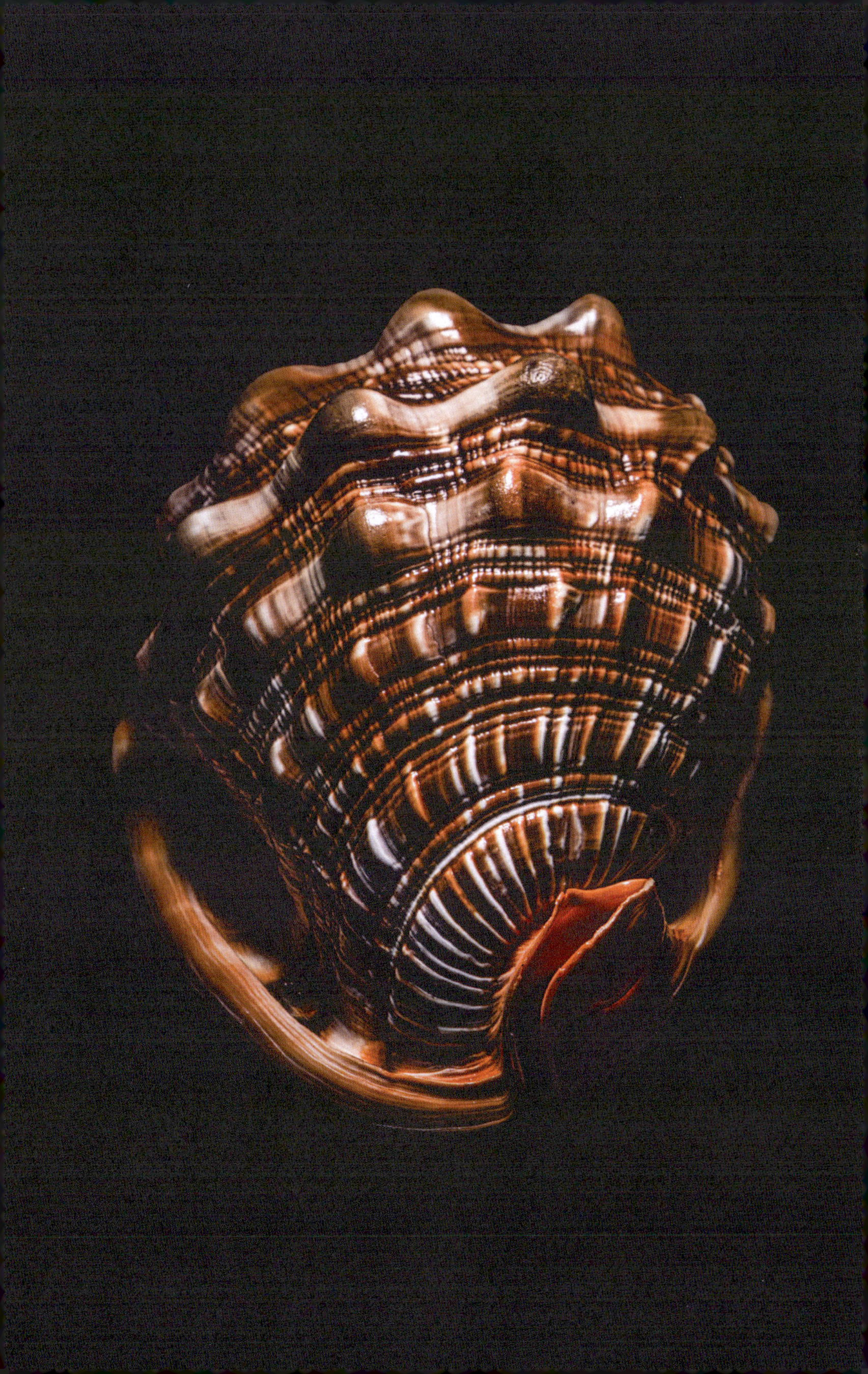

The resulting fatigue is then answered with more coffee, and so the cycle continues. Chocolate has a similar effect.

The capacity to respond to illness appears markedly improved in studies of people who drink coffee. People will report that concentration is improved, headaches disappear, aches and pains disappear, that all manner of diseases improve. These responses are courtesy of the expenditure—the combustion—of something very precious. Each time the adrenal glands are activated for entertainment, or cheap top-up energy, another little cell of your deep battery is emptied. This is our actual longevity that is being squandered. We only have one battery, and it includes the kidneys and adrenal glands. When that power runs out, we become unable to deal with illness. The good news is that we can begin to replenish that lost potential with dedication to the kinds of things I'm talking about in this book.

I once had a patient who hadn't slept more than four hours a night for two years. He did not drink coffee. The insomnia lined up exactly with the time he began a new job. I asked many questions about the job: was he happy there, did he like his boss, was it fulfilling, etc. Eventually it was revealed that every morning one of the workers would pass around her glass jar of chocolate-coated coffee beans. My patient hadn't made the connection that this could affect his nighttime sleep. When I suggested the connection, he still balked: "Then why do I still sleep badly on the weekends?" The answer is that the nervous system cannot get back on track quickly after such overstimulation. Once he gave the habit up and had a few helpful treatments, his sleep returned to normal.

Another patient reported that she developed migraines every day unless she had her morning iced coffee. We worked out that she frequently "forgot" to eat, causing her liver to tighten and the gallbladder channel to seize, leading straight to a daily migraine. The migraine led to the "need" for another coffee, and hence the continuation of the daily cycle. A dramatic increase in her food and fluid intake eliminated the migraines (without weight gain) and the coffee habit fell away.

26. Guilt-Free Eating

Sometimes a patient will say something like, "I was eating a piece of chocolate cake and your voice was in my head talking about my diabetes, and I felt so guilty but I ate it anyway, and afterward I felt very unwell."

Guilt is a constricting emotion that slows digestion and can do just as much damage as ill-advised food. Make a pact with yourself to thoroughly enjoy everything you eat. Look at it and love the way it looks. Smell it and love the smell. Touch it and love the texture. Put it in your mouth and really taste it and love the taste. Chew it and love the sensation of chewing it. Prepare the next bite and love it thoroughly all over again with all your attention. Enjoy it with every cell of your being. Don't eat anything without putting your full attention on it. You will find two things happen: first, you'll enjoy your food so much more, and second, eventually, you will be unable to eat what your body cannot love.

27. Clear the Burners

Leave garlic and chili out of your diet. Garlic has a reputation for blood purifying, having been used for millennia in Chinese herbal medicine as an incinerator of blood toxins, but it can do that only because it generates enormous heat. Therefore, even in the worst of cases, its best use is strictly short-term. Continued frequent use of garlic will ultimately dehydrate the body and create digestive problems such as heartburn and stomach ulcers. Garlic supplements are made from concentrated dried garlic, amplifying the heat exponentially.

Garlic is one of the most misunderstood plants. It's an extremely hot herb, not a food, and certainly not a supplement. Consumed over time, garlic will create an enormous amount of heat in the stomach and in the digestive tract in general. Gradually this heat can consume the healthy lining of the stomach. Heat accumulated in digestion can rise to the heart and lungs, creating palpitations and inflammation, which then is met with phlegm that the body duly manufacturers to subdue the heat. This creates a fusion of phlegm and inflammation called damp-heat which is sticky and difficult to eliminate. Eventually the face will become very red and the eyes perhaps bloodshot.

For people with a red complexion, high blood pressure, tinnitus, tremors, dizziness, frequent headaches or migraines, garlic is plain dangerous. Chilis and other peppers are very hot, too. If you really love garlic, savor it in a dish on special occasions, as a treat.

I had a patient once who came to the office after recovering from thyroid cancer. Although the cancer was cleared, he was still vomiting regularly and had migraines and mild seizures. I found his pulses to be extremely rapid, a sign of great inflammation. After some questioning about where this heat might be coming from, and after denying that he ate garlic, he mentioned as an aside that he was taking two garlic capsules with every meal. He also put hot sauce on "everything", even breakfast. The garlic and the hot sauce

had so dehydrated him and created so much heat that his blood and fluid volumes had dropped far enough to create wind (instability) that in turn produced the projectile vomiting, visual migraines, and seizures. The original thyroid problems he had experienced were corruptions of last-ditch attempts to create blockages to the heat reaching the brain. We removed the hot sauce and garlic from his diet, and with acupuncture treatments to remind his body to descend qi, all the symptoms ceased.

I first visited Naples in the late 1990s. I had left Australia to emigrate to the United States and spent three months in Europe with Andrew on his long tour with Philip Glass, wending our way through a dozen countries. It was thrilling to be out there with my new fiancé without owning a single key—a sense of complete freedom. In every city we visited, one of our favorite things to do was walk off the beaten track to find tiny family restaurants with no signage and no menus. These were gems, where often the parent cooked, and a son or daughter waited tables. In the back blocks of Naples beneath lines of drying laundry slung crisscrossed between buildings was Gino's place—five tables with blue plaid cloths, each with four seats. There was no menu and not a word of English, so we knew we were in for a treat. We were the first there for lunch and Gino didn't know the menu so he called out to the kitchen. The cook yelled back a short list and very soon the first dish came out, and the others followed over the course of an hour. We hadn't tasted food that good, perhaps ever. The most spectacular of all was the simplest—a small bowl of perfectly cooked pasta with the perfect amount of exquisite olive oil, just the right salt and a hint of peperoncino. Andrew urged me to ask Gino whether he could tell us how such a well-known dish was prepared to be so special. He immediately called out that we were coming into the kitchen. The cook wasn't Gino's mother—she was his grandmother. La Nonna was probably born in the 1920s and a great teacher, holding nothing back. Her every movement was elegant, gentle, and quick and what was most noticeable was her respect and love for the food. Every ingredient was caressed and greeted with a quiet joy. She inhabited every moment with a committed presence, focus, and a deep sense of purpose. It was a huge lesson. She put some fine pasta in a boiling pot and heated a small pan. Then with the graceful flick of a knife she took the skin off a clove of garlic, poured a little olive oil in the pan and threw in the clove, whole. Then she turned to me and said that it was extremely important to stir the garlic around the pan no more than three times and then to throw it out. I asked her why three and she said that three is enough, that garlic is strictly only for its perfume and that it is not food. The oil would hold just the right amount of perfume with three stirs. Never eat it, she said. You must throw it out. She put a tiny peperoncino into a mortar and ground it into little flecks and with a few deft movements, the pasta left the pot, landed in the pan with some of the peperoncino for a few seconds and then was tossed into the bowl. "Eat it hot and it's worth everything," she said. We chatted for a while and she told me she had never left Naples, she'd never stopped cooking, and she was happy I wanted to learn because she wanted to pass on as much knowledge as possible. It was a magical time spent in one of the most special kitchens I've been in. It was then that I learned that good cooking is not about fancy techniques, flashy recipes, or complex sauces; it's about fresh ingredients, grace, subtlety, and a reverence for food.

28. Notice Everything

Reflect on the changes each meal makes in your body. This educates you in terms of what's appropriate for your body. Many times patients will say something like, "Whenever I eat wheat, I feel tired," or, "Whenever I eat onions I get terribly embarrassing gas," or, "Whenever I have ice cream my nose runs," or, "Whenever I eat in a hurry I feel terrible for a whole day," or, "When I eat dessert I feel as though I never digest my main course," or, "When I drink something cold, I always cough," or, "When I eat lemons I get a headache," or, "Whenever I eat scallops my mouth has a weird tingling sensation." Every person has a different set of tolerances, aversions, and needs. Your body is giving you lessons and clues constantly about what it does not want. Listen carefully – you'll know much more about how to treat your body, and you'll be much healthier.

Many people reach for antacids or acid reflux medications to ease a feeling of indigestion. These substances block normal acid secretion in the stomach. As a result, protein foods that require stomach acid for digestion are left incompletely digested. When the small intestine repeatedly receives food that cannot be absorbed, the walls of the gut become inflamed and eventually leaky. At that point, the blood receives particles that it shouldn't yet have. This creates inflammation in the circulatory system, leading ultimately to damp-heat in the blood and lymph, often seen as cardiovascular disease.

If you have indigestion or a variety of acid reflux, it is crucial to discover its causes, dietarily, emotionally, and if you have the tools, energetically. Notice what foods irritate your system and replace them with calmer, different foods. If it's a cooking method that upsets you, such as frying, steam or bake your food instead. After cooking, add a little olive oil and a little salt to make it just as delicious. Many people come to realize that the offending food is one that they've been eating habitually for years. This is common with onions, for example. Other people realize that they are eating in a hurry and are not relaxed when eating, or not chewing enough. The dietary causes of reflux can be many. Listen carefully and really hear what your gut tells you. Reflux can also result from resistance to life—existing in an unpleasant situation when you know that surely things could be better. Change is key to health.

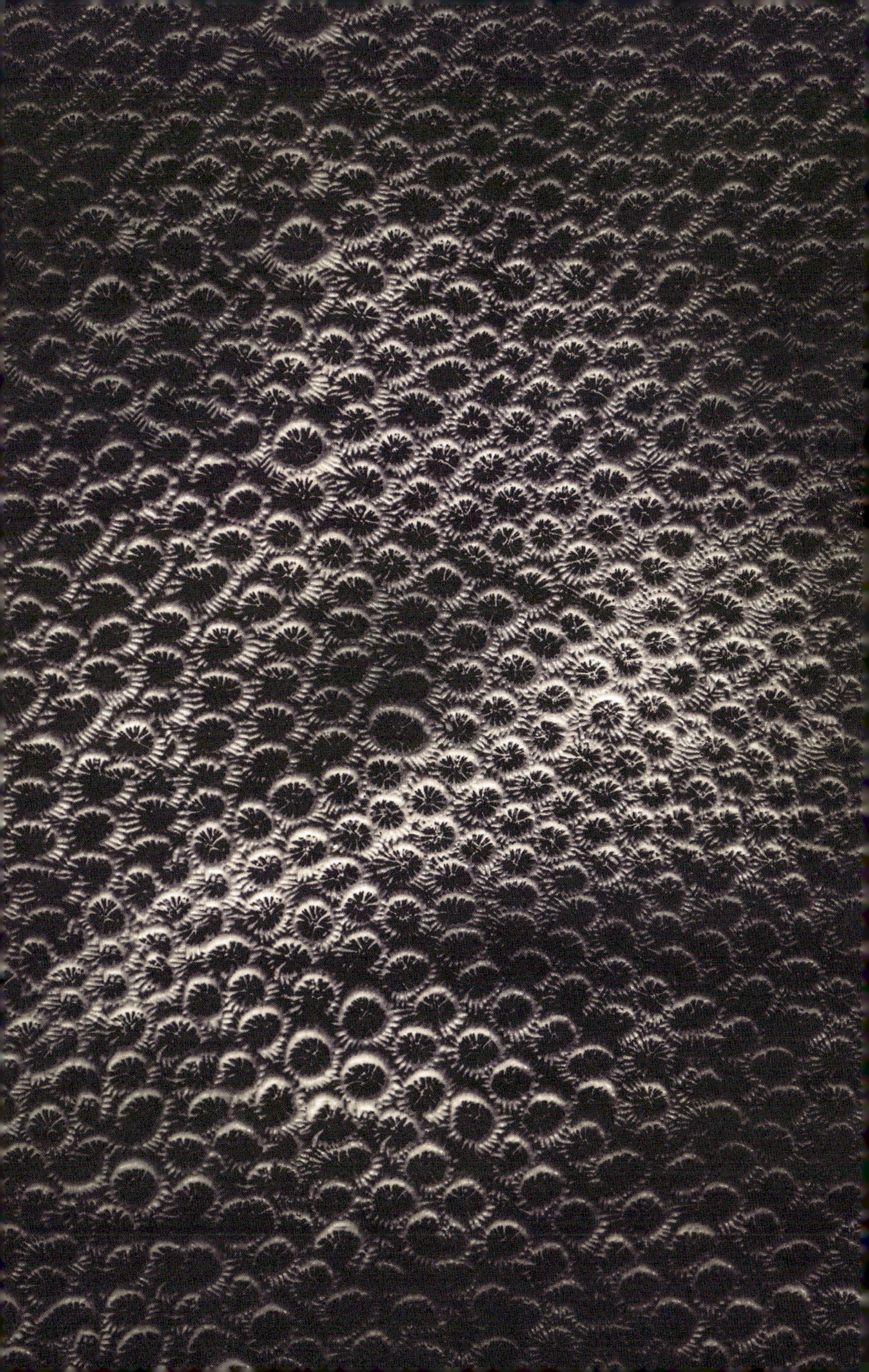

29. Don't Be Rash

Rashes are often avoidable. In the office I see people who are quite distressed about rashes. It's important to remember that the body does not make errors. Almost every annoying thing you experience your body doing is a response to a challenge it didn't ask for.

Rashes are the body's attempt to eliminate inflammation through the skin. The task of the physician is to determine the cause of the inflammation. Usually the cause is a food, but it can also be other things such as chemicals in certain laundry detergents, cleaning supplies and bleach; additives in dryer sheets, deodorants, moisturizers, perfumes, cosmetics, dyes, starches, hair products, hand lotions; and soaps, sanitizers and disinfectants for everything, or even chemicals that are released from furniture and carpets. Sometimes people become completely accustomed to the problematic chemical smells in their home and are utterly bewildered when I can name the type of product I can smell on them when they come in for a treatment. This is too much chemical interference.

We don't need most of the products we use, but have fallen prey to advertisers who tell us that we are unclean if we do not. Every chemical you can stop using is one less thing to which your body needs to mount a reaction. Choose simple home cleaning and grooming products, with sensible ingredients and as few additives as possible. And consider baking soda and household vinegar for cleaning many things. They are cheap and extremely effective. Eliminate what is unnecessary. Breathing chemicals in all day and covering yourself in modern products is very challenging for the body. You might tolerate them for years and then suddenly reach the end of that tolerance at which point you can find yourself with rashes, asthma, palpitations, even anxiety as the liver overworks to clear these unnatural toxins, and tightens in the process.

Sometimes people come in and they have already worked hard to research and eliminate the toxins they were living with in their space and in their hygiene habits, and yet they still experience rashes. Then we know that there is likely a dietary explanation. In my clinical experience, foods that are extremely yang (having a hot and moving energy) will often cause the body to try to vent that heat through the skin. These foods can include shrimp, crab, lobster, chicken breast, hot spices, garlic, bulb onions, and to a lesser degree some game meats when overeaten. Shrimp, crab, and lobster are exoskeletal shellfish, meaning they have a vector to the skin and that vector is one of strong protection. Eating those foods conveys that energetic signature to your body, causing it to move defensive qi to the exterior. This qi is hot, especially when gathered at the exterior, in fact it overlaps with the qi that fevers are made from.

Chemical allergies and rashes can result from food that was grown from GMO seed, treated with pesticides, herbicides, or was processed with additives to preserve, color, and stabilize it. Any food that is rancid (as supermarket nuts sometimes are) can cause rashes. Buying organic food is fortunately becoming less expensive, but organic laws have exceptions and loopholes, allowing some use of unwanted substances. We have to shop with a keen eye not only for freshness but commercial manipulation and food alteration. Some smaller farms avoid the official organic label while setting their own standards above what is required for organic certification. When you can, look for these exceptional farms in your area that are refusing to use any chemicals at all—loving the land, the produce, the livestock, and the work. The produce is sometimes more expensive, but it tastes amazing and is an investment in individual health and in the future of humanity.

Nearly always, when all the factors above are removed, rashes simply disappear. There is another issue, though, that challenges the skin, and that is deep unhappiness about one's environment. If you are in a job, a home, a marriage, a relationship, a country, a situation that you cannot tolerate, your exterior can generate rashes as a metaphor for pushing your environment away. As the

faithful deliverer of messages from the unconscious mind, the body doesn't lie. This I see quite often because I treat people with seemingly intractable conditions. Often these people have tried everything, removed all irritants and even made the drastic step of taking steroids, to no avail. When I ask how things in general are going, the dam breaks—the outpouring of deep unhappiness with an important aspect of life. There are many ways to enact release of illness if we understand how illness arises. Each way requires noticing what is constraining us, making changes even if they are difficult, and being committed to a more expansive way of thinking and living.

30. Running Ragged

Walk, don't run! The act of running triggers a hard-wired primitive brain message of danger. The brain responds to running as though your survival is at risk—why else would you be running? The adrenal glands are activated; giving a feeling of strength and endurance, ensuring and even encouraging you to free yourself from danger.

Running taxes the energetic mechanisms of the kidneys, potentially leading to premature aging and weakening of the immune system over time, since kidney qi finances immunity. Running also places great stress on the energetic mechanisms of the heart. Brisk walking, swimming, rowing, and cycling are fine substitutes for running's pounding punishment on the skeleton. These are all rotational exercises. (Yes, walking, too, is rotational if you allow your hips to move naturally.) Rotational movements are much more gentle on the precious body.

31. Liver Jam

Finish eating for the day as early as possible. If your liver is nice and relaxed, with every heartbeat during sleep, a larger than usual portion of your blood goes to the liver. This extra blood traffic to the liver is part of the mechanism of dreams. If you've eaten within a couple of hours before going to bed, however, your liver is fully occupied, and still working to help digest your food. Not only will your sleep be comparatively shallow, but dreaming—which requires a relaxed liver—cannot be full and open. You'll wake up feeling slightly unsettled, or even heavy and listless and slightly less optimistic, and not know why. Dreaming resolves the issues of the day and prepares you to wake with a clean slate.

Don't worry if you don't remember your dreams. Ideally your dreams are resolved during sleep and there is no need to remember them unless they are instructional. Keep a notebook at your bedside to note those special dreams down before they disappear.

If you must eat late, eat protein. Protein is digested in the stomach. Carbohydrates are mainly digested farther down the digestive tract, in the small intestine. A meal of mixed protein and carbs during the day is fine (unless your gut is particularly weak, in which case separation may be beneficial). A meal of carbs will sit in your stomach for a while and then spend a long time in the small intestine where the digestive process is slow. The small intestine has a close relationship with the center of the chest. If the chest interior cannot relax because the small intestine is busy, sleep cannot be deep. If you really must eat late at night, let your stomach handle some protein to get the bulk of the digestive process over with more quickly. It's infinitely better, though, to finish eating at least two hours before going to bed, so that the entire digestive tract is calm.

32. Wired and Bound

See fatigue clearly. Are you pushing yourself beyond your limits and brushing aside the feelings that result in your body and mind? Do you feel as though you could fall asleep any time between three p.m. and six thirty p.m.? Do you make errors and then steel yourself to do better? Do you experience subtle waves of fatigue and force yourself to keep going? Do you feel that occasionally your limbs or fingers just don't want to do what you're asking them to, but you push though that feeling and do it anyway? Do you sometimes get little twitches in your eyes or muscles? Do you find yourself more energetic late at night and have trouble falling or staying asleep? Do you feel you can't keep up without caffeine? If any of these things are true for you, you are tired. Declare to yourself that you are tired. That will release the pressure of pretending that you are brimming with energy. Go to bed as early as you can for as many days or weeks as you need until you feel refreshed on waking, and wakeful during the day. The reason you can get a "wired" feeling at night is that you've been running on adrenaline for so long that it's habitually stimulated, and you can't really calm down. Eliminate as many stresses as you can. Perhaps you are engaged in constant minor arguments. Perhaps you are living with a host of minor annoyances. Perhaps you take your work home, or work at home and never put it away. Perhaps you have a sick person in the household, or an elderly person to care for on top of your job. Perhaps you are looking at unsettling content on social media and are becoming stirred up without even realizing. Delegate more if you can and create boundaries as best you can to free time for more rest, and then commit to true resting, instead of being constantly occupied. You will be of far more help to those around you because you'll have the energy to spare, and enthusiasm will arise more easily. Take care of yourself by claiming your rest time.

33. The Doze Point

During the evening there's a time I like to call the doze point—the time you say to yourself, "If I were to lie down right now, I would fall asleep straightaway". After the doze point, the extra qi you call upon to remain awake is financed by your adrenal glands, a part of what we call kidney yang, the essential moving and warming qi that is part of your deepest energy reserve. If it were easily replaceable, it wouldn't be a problem to spend that energy, but the capacity to activate kidney yang qi is finite. Natural death arrives when kidney yang runs out. So staying up past the doze point costs one dearly. People who routinely go to bed very late age quickly. They also suffer from issues related to depleted kidney yang: problems with digestion, vision, concentration, immunity, etc.

Most people don't even notice their doze point. They ignore it or push right past it. Or they might be engaged in something very stimulating that activates adrenaline and prevents the doze point even emerging. Turn your lights down, and turn down the brightness of all devices and try to wean yourself off devices at nighttime.

Ignoring this signal to sleep and therefore running on adrenaline causes you to wake up feeling unrested, perhaps resentful of having to drag yourself out of bed. You are likely a snooze button hitter and you swear that it's normal to be dependent on coffee in the morning.

Going to sleep right on that signal for a while will change your life immensely. You can wake up refreshed, rested, and genuinely enthusiastic, or at least more optimistic about the day and its challenges.

To find your doze point, eat dinner early, then go through your getting-ready-for-bed routine and lay your sleep clothes out, ready to put on. This is an action—or even a ritual—that signals your intention to notice the doze point. Carry on with your evening activities (hopefully they are restful) and all the while, be very aware of your consciousness. Listen to your body and your mind. When you feel you could nod off, when you feel you'd love to close your eyes, when you feel the tiniest bit sleepy, put your sleep clothes on and get into bed and straightaway close your eyes.

Often when I get to this point in the sleep lesson, the patient says to me that it's utterly impossible to do this because they have so much to do. "What if my doze point is at eight p.m. and there are so many emails to read and answer, so much news to catch up on, and the desire for some entertainment?"

The artistic types will invariably say, "Totally impossible!

I do my best and most creative work and I get my best ideas well after midnight."

This is an interesting phenomenon. Why might this be so? Kidney yang, which as we know includes adrenaline, is not only moving and warming qi, it's also our core creative qi, responsible not only for reproduction but for creating anything. When you stay up past the doze point, your body assumes you are in danger. This is because our natural wiring is ancient, dating from the earliest humans, an eon before the electric light. We are wired to go to bed with the setting of the sun and to rise with the sun. When we are awake long after sunset and push ourselves through fatigue, the body assumes there is a threat to existence. A threat to life generates adrenaline so that the mind can think creatively and fast in order to escape from danger. It enables you to work out how to get past the snake, how to navigate around the grass fire, where to shelter from the thunderstorm, where to run to very fast. When you're safe at home passing the doze point and that surge of kidney yang hits you, creativity is stirred, and creative thought emerges as if like magic. There's a kind of excitement along with it, making the dark of night enthralling, magical, ripe with ideas. The only problem with this scenario is that the energy being used is coming from your deepest reserve and is very expensive. It's not coming from the food you ate that day; the qi from that day's meals is trying to get you to stop. Living in this way will never lead to a feeling of being rested and grounded.

Interestingly, many artists or writers will tell you that when they look at their work the next day, it doesn't seem nearly as good as it did the night before.

There's another time during the day that this creative force of kidney yang is naturally arising without the artificial rush, and that is early morning. When the sun rises, light stimulates the eyes to open. A shot of kidney yang opens the eyes and at the same time, theoretically, there emerges a shot of enthusiasm for the day. It's at this time that creativity is naturally at its relaxed best. This is true creativity time. You may find that after making this major adjustment, you do your very best work early in the day.

If you consider yourself a late-night person, you have worked your way into being automatically geared to feeling unlike yourself in the morning. While it might actually be that you really do have "night person" as a personality trait, usually it is simply an attraction to the feeling of adrenaline. Many of my patients have shifted from being night to being morning people, including artists, and they report that life goes on, and goes on better.

34. Cradleless Phone

Look at your phone in the living room, not in bed. Beds are for sleeping, resting, and loving. That's it. The vibration of a space is set by the activity that occupies it. If you stare at your phone in bed, your mind gets the idea that bed is a good place for the brain to be active, and you might have difficulty falling asleep easily, or sleeping well without waking. Some people find the opposite to be true—they say they get sleepy quickly—but these people are usually overtired. In order to improve sleep, dedicate the bed to just rest, love, and sleep.

35. Sea Change

Reflect on the changes that each activity has on your body. After you've had a conversation on the phone with a certain person, do you feel heavy or wiped out? After you've spent time in the presence of a certain person, do you feel depleted, and yet, after you've spent some time with a different person, you feel energized and restored? After taking a walk do you feel calm? After a bath? Does sitting in a certain chair bother your back? Do your eyes or your temples hurt or twitch after you've been looking at a screen for a certain period of time? Does your ankle get a cramp when you wear a certain pair of shoes? Do you get cold after a shower because you don't dress straight afterward? Are you walking around your home with cold feet? Are you straining your neck to look at your computer screen? Do you dislike your pillow? Does your shampoo make your head itchy? Is the sound of your alarm clock irritating? Is your car seat uncomfortable, causing you to hold your body a certain way? Does your bedroom blind annoy you because the streetlamp shines straight through a gap?

Many people go about their day unaware of the energetic impact a given activity or thing has on their body or mind. They feel that they are fortunate even to have a roof over their heads and a job to go to and a chair to sit in, and that it is not appropriate to complain. Naturally, I agree. What I'm referring to here are small adjustments to enable the body to give up its defenses. Our homes should be places where we can put our defenses down, and that would be good at work, too. Being strong and remaining aware doesn't require having our defenses aroused, even in subtle ways. Start with small things.

During and after an activity or encounter, focus on how you're feeling in mind and body. Take a moment to notice. In many instances, you can choose a new way and be much more comfortable, much more at ease. When the body is in a position of having to compensate for or defend itself, it uses valuable energy, leaving you less vital

than you could be. Maybe a cushion on that chair or in the car would prevent you holding your neck in a way that gives you a headache. Slippers or socks will warm your feet and prevent the consumption of vital kidney energy. Changing that friendship or making a new friend instead of becoming exhausted by that draining "friend" will elevate your energy. Temporarily tacking an old scarf up over the gap in the blinds will let you finally get a good night's sleep. Small things like this calm the immune system down, freeing so much energy for other things. And choosing what's best for your mind and body is usually what's best for those around you, too.

36. Extra Zs

Get a little more sleep than you think you need. We live in a chronically under-slept culture. Due to distraction, overwork, and time demands, sleep for many is a short-supply commodity. When your body is deprived of sleep, many things suffer: optimism, resilience to disease, mental stability, digestive function, suppleness, hormonal balance, and perhaps the most important, hydration and its dependent: longevity. Sleep maximizes the regulation and manufacture of any bodily fluid. The immune system is entirely dependent on available fluids to purge waste, toxins, and pathogens through sweating, sneezing, coughing, urination, defecation, vomiting, even bleeding.

Dehydration threatens all these immune responses, making illness vastly more likely. Drinking water is important, eating wet foods is important, but sleep is the clincher: sleep puts fluids into balance.

The old notion of the body needing eight hours sleep aligns with Chinese medicine wisdom. So many things that can't be measured happen during sleep, including the internal preparation needed to wake up refreshed and energetic. It is during the seventh and eighth hours of sleep that the internally circulating healing qi returns to the kidneys. The kidneys are then primed to produce the small amount of stirring charge that's released as the eyes open in the morning, stimulating natural enthusiasm for the new day.

Your body is hoping to be in rest mode from sundown onward. You probably won't want to go to bed then, but the body wants to begin to wind down. Subtract the number of hours you feel you need to sleep (minimum of eight) from about six a.m. which is a general time your body is likely to begin coming out of rest mode. The earlier you go to bed, the better and deeper the quality of rest you have because the body has not had to engage yang qi (adrenaline in this case) to try to stay awake, to be artificially excited. If you find it difficult to go to bed early, inch your bedtime forward progressively by ten minutes each night until you get to your optimum time. Your body wants to begin nourishing its substance and fluids (known as yin) during the late evening hours and it can't do that if you're not asleep. Going to bed early will make your body much more supple and moist, leading to smooth skin, calm digestion, better quality of sleep, a more hydrated system, more energy, and a healthier and longer life.

37. Rewind

When you go to bed at night, run through your entire day, backward. This simple method is the beginning of a full spiritual practice, written about nearly two thousand years ago in the work of the early Daoist alchemist named Ge Hong. Going through the events of the day when you lie down at night enables the unconscious mind to process them, reducing the amount of processing needed in the dream state. In a way, this allows the unconscious to cut to the chase in the dream state, expanding consciousness rather than play catch-up on mind healing. Begin by replaying the last thing you did before going to bed and end with holding in your mind a picture of yourself asleep that morning. By the time you get there, you'll probably already be asleep and you'll sleep more deeply.

38. Nighttime Defrost

Sleep without the air conditioner. Defensive qi, which protects the body from invasion by pathogenic factors of cold or wind, moves inside to the center of the chest to protect the heart during sleep. Because defensive qi has moved off the surface of the body, you are far less able to ward off a cold during sleep. The cold breeze from a window or an air conditioner can breach your immune defenses easily, causing you to develop a stiff neck or catch a cold.

In the summer months in New York City, the number of back and neck injuries I see increases dramatically. I call these "AC injuries" because upon questioning, it usually turns out that these patients have been sleeping in the cold draft of the modern, air-conditioned summer bedroom. If you must use the air conditioning at night, put it on a very gentle setting and be sure that there is no active breeze blowing to your body.

39. Peace Corps

Try to stay as relaxed as possible and not engage in confrontation. The energy that flows through the liver and gallbladder is responsible for distributing vital energy throughout the muscles, tendons, and ligaments.

The liver is also the target of stress responses, causing it to tighten, hence the old expressions: "She's bilious!" (meaning ill-tempered) or "He gets my bile up" (makes me angry), or, "But I am pigeon-livered and lack gall" (from Shakespeare, meaning weak when challenged). If the liver is distracted and constricted due to prolonged stress, it cannot properly distribute energy to the muscles; the body will become more and more stiff. Avoiding unnecessary confrontation and repetitive disturbing news will increase your suppleness, making you more able to weather the stresses that are unavoidable.

40. Daybreak

Spend some time every day being quiet. Quiet time resets the mind and allows a new perspective to emerge. New perspectives initiate new interests, inventive thinking, course corrections, and allow for resolutions of conflict. A little time without distractions or entertainment is invaluable for everyone, and even a short time can be transformational. It need only be five minutes at first—time with eyes closed, just focusing on breathing. Expand your breath by widening your chest as you breathe in and out and focus on the idea that you can allow more space in your life. When you begin to notice how much clearer you feel and how much more productive you are as a result, you'll start doing it more frequently.

If you start to treasure this time, consider spending time being quiet in a warm bath which you might find even more relaxing, or even doing some meditation. Meditation is an innate skill. All that is required is time to concentrate on the action of breathing in and out. The goal isn't so much to live without stresses as to gain a new perspective on them—one of less frustration and anxiety. Eventually we begin to lose interest in what bothers us.

My husband was awarded an honorary Ph.D in Daydreaming from a prestigious university, but he missed the ceremony.

41. Postprandial Pace

Breathe slowly after eating. There is a saying in Chinese medicine: after eating, we should "rest and digest". One reason is that the action of breathing gently descends stomach qi; it helps the contents of the digestive tract move downward. If we're overly active, this descending action is reduced and digestion can stall or slow, creating many different problems. Slow breathing is one of the great hidden secrets. It's so easy, so obvious, and yet all of us could do a bit more. We don't even need any equipment, special clothing, or special coaching. Over time, this practice leads to a compounding calm.

Breathing deeply will be a natural result of slow breathing practice. Apart from providing your body with oxygen, the act of breathing deeply has a profound healing action. As you breathe, the diaphragm (the muscle that sits between your lungs and abdomen) moves down and presses gently on your internal organs. This constant massage aids peristalsis (rhythmic movement of food through the gut) and also massages the liver, as the liver sits directly below the diaphragm. This keeps the qi of the entire digestive tract moving in harmonizing motion.

Acupuncture, massage, gentle exercise, and meditation can dramatically enhance the quality of your breathing. To practice deep breathing, sit calmly and, with every breath, allow your abdomen and chest to expand at the same time. Imagine the breath moving to below your navel. You'll feel more balanced, relaxed, open, and peacefully aware.

42. Align to Streamline

Maintain good posture. Open, free communication between your chest and your lower abdomen is crucial for good reproductive system health and for fertility. When you slump in your chair, the energy flowing through your center mid-line including the xiphoid process (the little bone at the bottom of the breastbone) presses inward, hindering the free flow of energy between your chest and reproductive system. Every breath should complement the qi of the uterus, ovaries, and prostate. Shallow breathing, often caused by poor posture, is detrimental to this region.

If you work at a computer, be sure that you are relaxed and still in good posture. Release any tension by allowing your body to assume its natural position. When you hold part of your body out of its natural alignment, the rest of your body creates various compensations, leading to stress and tiredness.

43. Love Rules

Send love regardless. Life can be wonderful and it can also be frustrating. When we feel frustrated around someone, it can feel difficult or even impossible to send love to them. There is still a way to send love: simply put a hand over your chest and send love to your own heart. Things will feel more manageable, and a surprising number of things will change for the better.

44. Have Curriculum, Will Travel

Cultivate the idea that free will is a gift to enable you to choose how to occupy your life. In Chinese philosophy, each life begins with a curriculum. The energetic steppingstones of our path are, in a sense, already there, built in. Free will is about how we live out our predispositions. We can tackle the challenges with our choice of determination, fear, enjoyment, procrastination, denial, refusal, gusto, sadness, embitterment, pride—the list is endless. Continually reframing challenges as encoded messages of guidance helps us choose how to be, and to navigate more efficiently through life's maze and the additional challenges the mind constructs.

45. Sing Your Song

Do what you love. Even if you feel you can't earn a living doing what you love, do what you can of it anyway. Whether it's painting, gardening, mentoring, knitting, playing music, drawing, crafting, photography, dancing, cooking, singing, composing, woodworking, ceramics, writing, building, find some time to do something creative just for the sake of enjoyment. This is more important than most people realize. It opens and relaxes the heart, the center of joy. When the heart is relaxed, it is free to shine its light. This is why we are here.

We live in a culture where it's considered a victory to obtain a diagnosis and a medication to stop symptoms. We are barking up the wrong tree. It is better to eliminate the conditions that allowed the body have illness in the first place. In Chinese medicine the origin of all disease is said to originate in both the gut and the spirit. Injury to joyousness can create the urge to engage in a poor diet. Following one's heart is a cornerstone of health just as much as eating vegetables, or eliminating sugar.

46. Move Gut to Soothe All

Keep your digestive tract moving. A free moving tract is liberating on many levels because the qi that runs through the pancreas affects the musculature and also the mind. If the gut is moving well, relaxation emerges. The digestive tract slows down when laden with sugar, gluten, dairy, with foods that are sticky, processed, heavy, or cold, and when you've overeaten. It all becomes much worse when you're stressed or dehydrated. When the gut slows down, we call it stagnation, a term that is then differentiated into categories: stagnation of food, blood, qi, heat, cold, fluids and phlegm. Stagnations are focused in the three main regions: the chest, the middle abdomen, and the pelvis. Any of the stagnations can occur in any of the three regions. For example, blood stagnation in the pelvis could manifest as fibroids; cold stagnation in the chest might manifest as pain on breathing, tightness, or cough. In the middle region, phlegm stagnation could manifest as nausea or even projectile vomiting. Heat stagnation can show as ulcers, and fluid stagnation as swellings. Food stagnation is often the root of all other stagnations. It manifests first as indigestion, burping, hiccups, gas, bloating, or nausea. If your food is real food, unprocessed, and includes moistening dishes like soups and stews, the likelihood of any stagnation is vastly reduced, leading to a much more comfortable, immeasurably healthier life.

47. Sinus Security

Keep your sinuses clear by changing your food. If you feel stuffy in the sinuses, as though you'd really like to blow your nose but the congestion won't move, or if you have a long-standing or recurring sinus infection, or if you sometimes have postnasal drip or copious mucus coming from your nose, you most likely have a mucus or phlegm stagnation in the gut. Sinus infections occur when your gut is slowed down and exhausted by having to digest sugar, gluten, dairy, cold foods, raw or processed foods. This is because these are sticky, difficult to break down, or, in the case of processed foods, often not food

at all. The phlegm that is created in the digestive tract as a byproduct of these foods ends up being sent to your sinuses for eradication because if it is allowed to continue through the gut, it lines the gut and prevents the complete absorption of nutrients. This is why people with sinus blockages frequently report fatigue.

There's a saying in Chinese Medicine that blocked sinuses are the cause of a thousand diseases. This is because the mucus can trap all manner of irritants leading to perpetual issues as the sinuses are not draining. The immune system is constantly triggered, leading to frequent sneezing and the thickening of phlegm which eventually becomes yellow or green as the body activates heat to try to burn it up. You can irrigate the sinuses or do wonderful head steam baths and find some relief, but these measures will not treat the root cause. Once the root causes of blocked sinuses are eliminated, and hydrating foods are introduced, sinuses can recover quite quickly. Aromatic spices such as mint, shiso, cilantro, oregano, thyme, coriander seed, cumin, cardamom, and others can help with digestion and sinus health at the same time. This is a practice we refer to as working with the root and the branch of a problem at once.

Remember that fermented dairy is easier to digest than unfermented dairy and that butter does not contain dairy proteins and is therefore easy to digest for most people.

Both create less phlegm leading to less phlegm arising in the sinuses.

48. Longevity Hack

Cultivate your body's capacity to safely store what it cannot yet eliminate. The body is constantly dealing with the waste products of metabolism and with toxins or pathogenic factors that enter through the breath and the skin. It's also dealing with cold, which the body views as a pathogen. Physiological processes slow and stagnate in the presence of systemic cold.

As long as there is sufficient hydration—that is, sufficient fluid and blood volume—the eradication of toxins proceeds uninhibited, hopefully into the toilet, or through sweat, but sometimes as expulsions such as skin eruptions, as internal pollution sometimes seeks alternative exits.

If there is dehydration or low blood volume or a depletion of general resources, there is no vehicle to carry those waste products out. Instead, the body must relocate them to places where they can be kept quiet, away from the organs. The body is constantly working to protect the unobstructed function of the internal organs.

The body will hide toxins and cold inside joints, in fat, in spaces between bones and connective tissue, and other places where there is comparatively little circulation, all to keep the organs free of pathology and preserve life. Adequate hydration provided by a diet rich in fluids and that includes sufficient saturated fat allows the body to manufacture the substance necessary to move, sequester, and keep toxins quiet. If there are enough resources to perform these actions, the person experiences no symptoms at all; the pathogenic factor is said to be latent, or in remission. Pathogenic factors can be kept safely in hiding away from the organs for days, months, years or decades until the body regains the full hydration and the qi it needs to get rid of them. This sequestering is part of the body's indescribable genius.

There are three reasons to stay properly hydrated. First, you want to be able to keep these pathogenic factors at bay, tucked away in the joints where they can do little or no harm; fluid substance enables that to happen. Second, you don't want to add to your own pathogen stores—you want to maintain the vehicle of elimination which is also fluid. In other words, fluids are needed to support urination, defecation, and sweat. Third, if you do some really thorough work on hydration, your body can choose to let go of old stores of pathogenic factors and lighten its load because it registers that there is a vehicle present to carry it out of the body.

If the body becomes depleted and can't store pathogenic factors anymore, and at the same time there are insufficient fluids to carry them out, the toxins leach into the surrounding tissues. This often appears as arthritis, although it can manifest in hundreds of different diseases. We are taught that arthritis or these other "diseases of aging" are inevitable, but when we understand the path of causation, we know that aging doesn't need to equal illness. It's completely avoidable.

Proper hydration means increasing substance by including in the diet fluids and oils, including well-managed saturated fat. Fat is able to store toxins more than any other substance, and hence protects the internal organs. This is a key factor in staving off chronic degenerative diseases. Generous fat deposits exist deep in the abdomen around the viscera of all healthy people. Many of my patients with serious diseases are intentionally very thin and have lived a life of low-fat food, believing that they were doing the best for themselves. This misunderstanding, founded in faulty and debunked science, must stop. Avoid processed foods, including food stripped of its precious fat, and learn to cook simple inexpensive meals with simple ingredients. Avoid cold food, ice, cold drinks, stimulants, processed food, things with additives that are not food, and sugar. Your system needs real food and water. Question everything else you put into your body. It's a very precious vehicle designed only for clean air,

good food, and fresh water. Many ailments can simply fall away with this natural, comforting approach.

49. Limit to Expand

Today a patient came in and told me that he had successfully eliminated from his diet the few things we'd advised him were contributing to his illness. The list was short: wheat, cheese, tomato, sugar, and cold salads. He then lamented that he felt his diet had become unbearably narrow. In a case like his, almost invariably, the patient was going to the supermarket with his regular shopping list in mind, and returning home with items from that same list minus the foods on the "avoid" list—fewer foods than before! When you eliminate certain habit foods from your diet, your diet should expand. Become curious and courageous with food. Take home a vegetable you have never eaten before, or one you have no idea how to cook, or one that you didn't think you liked, or one that looks unusual to you. Try a grain you have never even heard of, like perhaps kaniwa or teff. There are thousands of foods you have likely never tried before that will contribute to your health, not your health issues.

50. Declutter to Decompress

Declutter your space to clear your mind. A clear mind is an important part of health. In Chinese Medicine, it's known that a person whose mind is constantly thinking and churning, or even just always distracted, eventually develops a weakened digestive tract. Digestive qi is responsible for clarity of thought, but the act of overthinking ultimately has a negative impact on your digestive function. This is where we get the phrase, "worrying yourself sick". More than just metaphor, clearing the mind of constant distraction contributes to health in a significant way. If your living space is cluttered, if it's full of things you don't need, your mind is cluttered with them, also. Everything you possess has a space in your mind. Consider your digestive issues connected in part to that. To declutter, set aside small amounts of time and go through one single drawer or one small area of your space each week. Then, give away or sell what you don't need, what you don't use, and especially what you don't like. If you want to be able to remember something you want to get rid of, take a photograph of it. Keep going until you've gone through your entire space, one short work session at a time so as not to become overwhelmed. Your mind will be much clearer and your spleen and pancreas much healthier, leading to a sharper mind, better digestion, healthier musculature, and improved circulation.

Consider returning all the things you borrowed and didn't give back. Everything you have holds a place in your mind. If some of those items that don't belong to you have the energy of needing to be returned to their owner, you will unknowingly not be at peace around those items. These unconscious tensions are significant and often completely unacknowledged. Either return them or make contact with the person who lent them and make it right. A part of you that was tense will relax.

51. Weave Your Trailing Tapestry

Release your grievances from your body. The energetic residue of everything you've experienced is stored in the channels we call the linking vessels. These conduits of energy record experiences both in your memory and in your body. If these channels are relaxed, the heart and kidneys communicate freely with one another—the kidneys transmitting to the heart this life's curriculum and the heart transmitting to the kidneys the gracious acceptance of life's mission. This conversation is the opposite of anxiety. The linking channels cannot be relaxed if life's experiences have not been processed. If there has been a trauma, whether mild or profound that has not been processed, and by that I mean has not been dealt with or spoken about but suppressed as the person has tried to forget it, the linking channel will be tight, stifling the communication between heart and kidneys, creating a constant feeling of being unsettled.

Most people think that they must forgive in order to be at peace, but it's really acknowledgment that it happened that is important. Once an experience is acknowledged and declared in the past, whether or not a person feels they can forgive, the linking channel is able to relax and weave that experience into the past, allowing the person to walk a clear path so that the experience is no longer hijacking the mind.

These incidents can range from a single verbal interaction; loss of a job, home, family member, or close friend; accidents, forced migration, separation, divorce, bankruptcy, abandonment, assault, starvation, theft, shocking movies, arguments that split families, photographs of violent scenes, finding a person dead, discovering affairs, holding grudges—the list of human experiences can go on. When successfully processed, they no longer prevent effective or successful living. The linking channels are the practical way these experiences are woven into a kind of energetic tapestry, a kind of record of your life. That record becomes part of a giant energetic library of all lives.

When traumatic experiences are not processed by the mind, when they are not able to move into the tapestry and become part of one's past, they can haunt one's thoughts, causing limitations to behavior and happiness.

One of the main reasons people hold trauma in their bodies is to keep a record of it. If, after the incident or experience, there was no healing, no punishment, no acknowledgment of what happened, no apology, no compensation, or if nobody believed it happened or nobody offered comfort—if there was no conclusion, then people can use their bodies as the record keeper and continue hurting in their bodies so as to be the container of the truth. The pain in the body becomes the evidence.

Acupuncture treatments of the inner linking channel, also known as yin wei mai, can help tremendously with trauma, but if acupuncture is not available, writing is effective. If you write down your grudges, your traumas, your regrets, your pain and your feelings, a certain freedom emerges in the body. This is because you've created a record of that trauma that can substitute for the body-record. Keep writing, perhaps twenty minutes every day, until it all runs out. As you experience the feeling of weight lifting off, you might be able to tolerate writing for longer periods. If you cannot write, record it into a phone or find a way to share it in a trusted space.

When you think you are finished writing, take your notebook and seal it all around with duct tape. Store it in a secret place. Your unconscious mind will know that there is a record and that it's locatable, leaving the mind free to release much of its tension. Declare that the burden you were holding in your shoulders and chest has been moved to your notebook, leaving you much lighter. In my practice this has proven to be powerful, life-changing, liberating medicine.

Trauma can create tightness in the muscles and connective tissues. Get somebody to massage you or do as much self-massage as you can. Acupuncturists can use sliding cups and gua sha (scraping techniques) that help release the physical hold over trauma.

52. Autopilot Clean

Do smart detoxes. Many people who think they are eating a very healthy diet are actually eating a depleting diet, meaning they are eating meals designed to drain things from their body. If you do this often, you could easily become cold and dehydrated. For example, a meal that includes lots of raw food (lettuce, tomato, cucumber, grated carrot, etc.) and perhaps accompanied by a green juice might be refreshingly cooling on the hottest of days because it will reduce body temperature, but if regularly eaten, these meals will trigger the body to urinate and

defecate more often than needed, taking some of the body's required hydration with it. The process also causes a depletion of qi. The net result is weight loss, dehydration, cold hands and feet, loose stools, trouble concentrating, decreased circulation and fatigue. Rather than schedule detoxes, become aware that bodies are cleansing and detoxing all the time, and all you need to do to have a cleaner interior is to stop putting toxins into it: processed foods, sugar, etc., remembering that the body is designed for water and food in as close as possible to its natural state.

53. Tomatoes, Bell Peppers and Eggplant

In the clinic, after I've advised the patient on changes they might make, the people who are deeply ill often say things like, "Don't hold back, tell me everything. I'm at the end of my rope, this is my last hope. I will do everything you tell me to do."

At that point, I often suggest they avoid nightshades (tomatoes, bell peppers, eggplant, and even white potato). They are not "first tier" foods to eliminate, but they are certainly problematic. Nightshades contain solanines—substances that are mildly toxic to the liver and affect the immune system, especially targeting the joints. In a person whose health is greatly challenged, the last thing they need is more taxation on the liver, which is best focused on storing blood and clearing toxicity. Often, when I list the nightshades along with gluten and cheese, the patient will say, "But that's my whole diet!" as if to say, "You want me to starve?" To which I answer as kindly as I can, "You can change your diet, or stay this path of illness." Then weeks later, as they report feeling immeasurably better, half of them ask when they may return to their beloved diet, to which I answer, "When you're ready to begin to be ill again." The other half say that they have completely lost their craving or taste for those foods. Being a clinician is an interesting exercise in nonjudgment. People are ready to make the big changes, or they're not ready, and both options are fine.

In the old days, nightshades were not considered foods. In Italy in the nineteenth century, you wouldn't dream of eating a tomato. They were popular ornamental plants, just as we have colorful plants we have around the home today. To throw a rotten tomato at a bad town square performer was the ultimate insult. But when Europe entered a deep depression with food shortages, people began to find ways to cook them. The methods developed were commonly in use until the 1980s. My best friend's grandmother (la Nonna) would visit from Italy for the summer months every year. The first thing she did was plant the garden—all nightshades. When the tomatoes ripened I would go over in the mornings on the weekends and watch her cook, listening to her instructions.

She would hold the tomato on a fork over a gas flame until the skin was scorched and then peel the skin off and throw it away. "Non per mangiare." (Not for eating.) Then she'd squeeze the seeds out into the sink. "Non per mangiare." Then she would cut up the tomatoes and put them into a pot and let them simmer on low heat all day long, until she used them in a sauce for pasta, or in a stuffing for eggplant or bell peppers. As it turns out, if you cook solanines for at least six hours, they break down and lose their toxicity. By contrast, canned tomatoes are pressure cooked for minutes. Their solanines are intact.

La Nonna would bake bell peppers. She'd hold the peppers over the gas flame until the skin blistered and charred and tear it off and throw it away. Then of course, the seeds came out. Then she would bake them with a vegetable or meat filling for a long time. Putting them in a salad raw was unthinkable.

Preparing eggplant was even more involved. She would char them, remove the skin and do a very light scraping over the seeds to try to get as many out as possible. Then she'd slice them quite thinly and lay them on large trays of salt for hours, turning them occasionally. Then she would take each slice and hold it under running water, as the solanines, absorbed by the salt, washed away. The slices would then be baked at fairly low temperature or layered as a lasagna and baked, covered, for hours. Slicing them and throwing them on the grill was unthinkable.

Nightshades originated in South America where the ancient method of cooking potatoes included burying them in coals in the ground for an extended time.

Each of these methods requires hours or work, traditionally done by grandmothers, as their offspring are busy with other work. These methods are probably not viable in our culture. But the unwillingness or the lack of time we have for cultivating true nourishment is costing us dearly in terms of health. If you have any kind of joint condition and you must eat nightshades, take your time on your day off and enjoy the connection to these foods and their cooking traditions. Prepare them in bulk and freeze them, perhaps. Otherwise, they are best left alone as the ornamental plants they were once considered to be.

54. Taste Buddy

Taste your food well. We have taste buds for good reason. Whatever is toxic offends them and we're moved to spit it out. While eating any food, the act of taste is intimately related to the depth of digestion. Long before the food descends to the gut, its taste is relayed to the intestines where the exact required proportion and type of enzyme and bacteria are assembled to meet the food and convert it into your individual being. The way in which food becomes each person has two broad facets: the actual digestive tract secretions that break down and transform food, and a subset of qi called da qi (heavenly qi). Da qi enters with each breath and carries with it the consciousness that enables the unique conversion of food to become that person. Da qi is enhanced and cultivated when the mind's focus during a meal is on its taste (and texture). It's then that the body breathes an entirely different way, bringing the qi of transformation deep into the digestive tract. When eating with distraction—that is, while watching a screen or typing a text, or while reading or being distracted by emotions—concentration is diverted away from tasting the food. Some people have reached the point where they barely notice what they are eating. The benefits of food are then vastly reduced.

One of the joys of being in Europe, in particular the Mediterranean countries, is experiencing the love of mealtimes when people sit quietly or happily or noisily with family and friends, enjoying being together eating simply and beautifully prepared food. There is always convivial conversation, including much discussion and admiration of the food itself. How superb the beans are today, and how tasty the artichokes, and how sweet the cherries are this year. Eating together and chatting around the table activates the heart—the seat of joy. The eyes and the tongue are on the heart's energetic channel. Eye-to-eye contact, and talking, and tasting food together, enliven and relax the heart. Enjoying meals with other people is not only quintessentially human, it's comforting, and good for digestion.

55. Ice Schmice

Warm your injuries. Use no ice. In Chinese medicine, injuries are treated as they would be if a baby were injured. Imagine putting an ice pack on a baby—it would be utterly shocking. And so it is with everyone—we've just become accustomed to the idea. Ice may bring swelling down, temporarily numb pain, and it may usher redness away, but it does so by limiting circulation to the area. Swelling occurs over injuries and bone breaks for two brilliant purposes: to immobilize the injured region so that the person does not do further damage through activity; and also to allow wei qi (the qi of the immune system) to gather at the site to begin the healing. Ice placed over this gathering will push the immune response inward, into the bone and/or the nearest joint, opening the risk of arthritis in later years, as the fusion of cold from the ice and warming immune qi eventually can damage the joint itself.

Currently, numerous sports teams are stopping all use of ice. And interestingly, the doctor who invented the ice-for-injuries protocol has strongly recanted it.

Since it is the immune system (wei qi) that detects changes

in barometric pressure and temperature, people who have a history of putting ice on injuries can often report that even years later, they can feel impending changes in weather "in my bones." This is because wei qi—which belongs at the exterior where it registers environmental changes—has been compressed inward by cold all the way to the joint, or to the bone where a fracture occurred. What about packs of frozen peas over an injury? Best to avoid. Instead, allow moderate swelling to occur as a natural part of healing, using acupuncture or herbal liniments to reduce extreme swelling and keep circulation moving.

To reduce the swelling of an injury, pinch the following points:

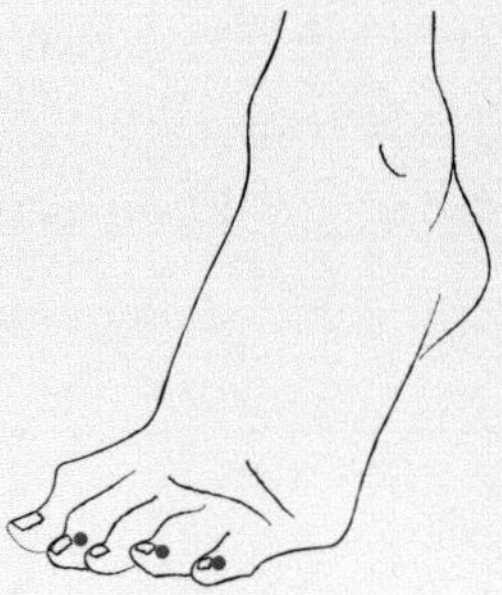

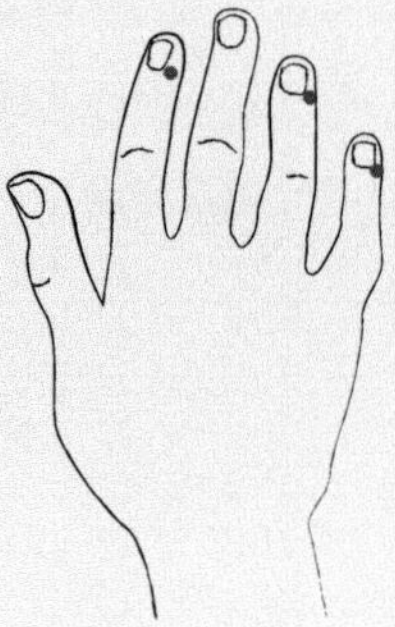

56. The Gut Whisperer

Be your own solar plexus whisperer. Your body is brilliant, infinitely wise, adaptable, forgiving, vibrant, and intelligent. It knows what to do and what help it needs, no matter what happens to it. If you listen to your body's wisdom, you will certainly be healthier. But what does it mean to "listen" to the body? The body speaks through the solar plexus, halfway between your navel and your heart. This region is connected to the heart by a channel we call the great connector of the stomach. Through this channel comes all inspiration, all original thought, all pure self-steering. Listening to the body means to feel into this region for guidance, rather than the mind. The mind on its own can only help repeat past behaviors, perhaps with variation. Inspiration and spirited change—true to one's unique course—comes not from the mind but from the gut. Action that is out of alignment with the gut is uncomfortable; it never feels quite right no matter how much your mind might insist it is so, but action that is in alignment with the gut feels comfortable in the body, even if the mind thrashes around in protest. Differentiating between the mind and the inner knowing associated with the belly is a cornerstone of health.

The Stones

Photographer Zohar Sterman has captured in these pages the essential beauty of the healing nature within stones. In the ancient Chinese medicine view, stones are living things with their own presence and influence. Along with the many suggestions for increasing health in this book, you might consider bringing a few stones into your living space, to help calm both environment and mind. We see the remnants of this understanding in our culture as it treasures gold and diamonds, but all stones and minerals are precious and have their own properties which can be used for personal healing.

Page 3: **Malachite**
Supports deep relaxation; its mineral content resonates with our living blood.

Page 7: **Apatite**
Prevents loss of energy.

Page 12: **Tiger's Eye**
Like all banded stones, supports the idea of sorting what is for us and what is not, a foundation both for digestion and meditative clarity.

Page 15: **Sulfur**
Quickens movement within, invigorating change and easing pain.

Page 22: **Selenite**
Purifies energies in a room, and helps complete recovery from illness.

Page 25: **Labradorite**
Has a way of enhancing intuition.

Page 30: **Jasper**
Has a way of promoting personal transformation.

Page 34: **Rhodochrosite**
Opens the heart.

Page 37: **Variscite**
Helps with physical trauma.

Page 42: **Pyrite**
Can shift stagnant energy to treat pain.

Page 47: **Conch Shell**
Shells are the strong protection for their hosts; they are deeply calming.

Page 52: **Opal**
Inspires us to loosen up and flow with life.

Page 57: **Coral**
Resonates with the ocean within, stimulating longevity and memory.

Page 61: **Blue Calcite**
Helps build a sense of belonging, aiding with anxiety.

Page 66: **Nautilus Shell**
As we perceive the outside world, we find hidden order, inspiring a sense of wonder.

Page 69: **Amethyst**
Soothes emotional wounds.

Page 74: **Boulder Opal**
Calms children and settles a restless fetus.

Page 78: **Desert Rose**
Can help us with developing abundance.

Page 81: **Pyrite Sun Disks**
Can ease depression.

Page 88: **Mookaite**
Assists us in moving through periods of change and transformation.

Page 93: **Double-terminated quartz**
Regulates energy and strongly amplifies the power of personal intention.

Page 100: **Mica**
Helps with bringing illness up and out, including the common cold.

Page 107: **Optical Calcite**
Helps us see the way through shyness and fear, with clarity.

Page 110: **Aquamarine**
Helps us to see the limitlessness of potential.

Photographer's Note

The power of photography as an art form has always been understated. Understated not only in the importance of art in healing, but also in the essence of photography itself. Artistically, a photograph can convey much more than light and color. If done well, a photograph can bring out the essence of a subject. A good landscape photograph can make you feel all the sensory things the photographer was experiencing at the moment of the shutter click; the humidity, temperature, the sweetness of the air, the smell of trees, the sound of the wind.

I grew up with the stones in this book, and by that I mean these stones were in our home, mostly on my windowsill, until I took them down and put them in front of my camera. I know these stones personally. I know the lively, deep wisdom of the amethyst, the masculine solidity of the pyrite, the slight rotten egg smell of the sulfur. When I photographed them, I didn't want to make them look pretty, I sought to capture the depth and personality of each stone. The photographs in this book are not ornamentation. Each photo will let you feel the energetic frequencies and spiritual properties of the stone. Living with these stones has given me a healing life, and my hope is that reading through this book—with its life changing content and the stones looking on—will be a healing experience for you as well.

Ravi Zohar Sterman,
Manhattan, 2023

Appendix 1

A Word about Acupuncturists

Good Acupuncturists and Channel Practitioners are able to assist with an astonishingly wide variety of disorders and diseases. Most people think of acupuncture as being only for pain management or relief from musculoskeletal problems and injuries, but acupuncture is far more than that.

Acupuncture can help with conditions ranging from a common cold to post-stroke paralysis; anything from nausea to Crohn's disease. Acupuncture is also a powerful method to address emotional stagnation and challenges.

Channel Practitioners and Acupuncturists who are trained in all the channels of acupuncture—the sinews, luos, divergent, eight extraordinary, and primary channels—can treat an even broader range of complaints including chronic degenerative diseases and severe emotional difficulties.

Channel Practitioner is a term applied to non-acupuncturists who are thoroughly trained in all the channels of acupuncture, but do not insert needles. In order to activate the channel they might use acupressure, essential oils, or stones. In many cases they will activate the channel remotely during or after communication with the patient on the phone or by video. Patients frequently report that remote treatment is so strong that they wish for nothing more.

Often, long lists of credentials are offered as sole markers of credibility. Focus instead on the view of the practitioner. I'm not talking here about style—I mean the way in which the practitioner functions in whatever style they practice. You're looking for a practitioner who understands that signs and symptoms are indicators of the body's responses to pathology and that symptoms are not the illness itself. You're looking for someone who understands how chronic degenerative diseases are reversible. It is a bonus if the practitioner you are considering uses all the channels of acupuncture: the sinew, luo, primary, divergent and eight extraordinary channels. Most important of all is sensing that the practitioner commits to acting with strong intention.

That means the practitioner:

- is kind.
- is optimistic.
- is focused.
- listens to you.
- is free of judgment.
- takes the pulses if you are in the same room.

- makes astute observations, and asks questions pertinent to you, rather than putting you through a set list of questions they ask of everybody.
- if in the same room, asks questions related to their pulse findings, rather than asking questions that may have nothing to do with you.
- makes unique diagnoses for each individual in each visit, and, if in person, takes your pulses in detail every visit.
- has confidence in your body's wisdom.
- after explanation, practices in warm silence, or with reassuring words about the treatment, or while explaining the meaning and function of the channel.
- practices with great concentration, patience, and reverence.
- above all, has strong, clear intention and maturity even if they are young.

Note: Steer clear of electric needle stimulation. Electric stimulation is a recent addition to the ancient art of acupuncture and introduces a single frequency in a one-size-fits-all mindset to a medicine in which treatment is radically individualized. This method disrespects qi as the body cannot detach from the stimulation when it is finished incorporating the invitation of that needle, leading to overstimulation of the point, often ruining the treatment. Without electro-stimulation, when the body is finished with a needle, it has the freedom to release its focus or grip on that needle, and sometimes even partially or completely push it out.
All acupuncturists should use single-use needles that are disposed of after each treatment.

If you visit an acupuncturist for pain due to injury, a good practitioner should not focus only on the physical location of the pain; rather the main focus should be on the most difficult movement for you. The answer to that question reveals the channel to which the injury has referred. Also essential for inclusion are exit points for pain which are located at the cuticles, whether in remote treatment or in person. If your pain worsens, ask that your acupuncturist use the sinew channels. The effective treatment of pain due to injury most often requires use of these channels. After treatment for pain, you should feel noticeably improved right away, even if just a hint at first, and significantly improved after seventy-two hours.

I offer a six-month training for people interested in becoming Channel Practitioners and for acupuncturists with any level of training or experience who wish to advance their skills in the practice of the channels—profound, intrinsic flowing fields of energy that have been used by acupuncturists for thousands of years.
For more information about the Channels of acupuncture and Classical Acupuncture in general, courses, blogs, articles, textbooks and other books, welcome to my website: www.AnnCecilSterman.com

Appendix 2

Cold Plunge, Cold Shower, Hot Mess.

Last week I saw a seemingly healthy, vibrant looking man in his late 30's presenting with particularly severe arthritis. All his joints were aching, especially hips, shoulders, knees and most of his finger joints.

How long have you had this joint pain?
Probably five years, maybe six.

What was happening in your life around that time?
Ummm, well, it was a great time and I'm having a great time now. I've been married happily for six years. My wife is a dream, the love of my life and we're planning to start a family next year.

Congratulations. How wonderful. How about your job?
I love my job and I own my own small company. It has its stresses, but whose doesn't!

What makes your joint pain feel better?
Holding a mug of hot coffee, actually.

Is it painful?
Yes, especially in the morning. I have trouble getting up. I feel like an old man.

Did you have health challenges as a child?
Not at all, totally healthy and active, and I was a college athlete, but I can't imagine even playing cards comfortably now.

Okay, thank you, let's take pulses.
(I examined the pulses at the wrist.)
Your pulses are very interesting and quite revealing. They're what we call tight pulses. Usually a tight pulse tells us that the body is trying to conserve a resource (blood or fluids) and we might find a tight pulse in one or two positions, but your pulses are tight all over and that leads me to certain types of questions. Is your low back tight?
Yes.

Do you have cold hands and feet?
Yes.

Do you sometimes feel cold to your core?
Yes, I guess. Sometimes I have chills.

Do you have gas and bloating?
Yes.

Do you sometimes get headaches?
Yes.

Do your symptoms come and go and are they worse on one side than the other side?
Yes. Wait, you can see all this from my pulses?

Well your pulses are clearly showing these things. You have a deep systemic cold and we have to find out why. Do you eat salads?
Yes, but just small side salads.

Do you juice?
No.
Do you sleep in air-conditioning or with a fan when it's too hot?
No.

Do you dress well enough to feel warm in this cold weather?
Yes. (He pointed to his heavy coat on the hook.)

Hmmmm, So this started six years ago and everything was going beautifully then, and continues to do so. I wonder what changed...
The only cold thing I do is my morning cold plunge. But that's to keep my immune system boosted. I had a cold plunge pool built right into my patio.

Oh! How does that boost your immune system?
Well the science is showing that when you do cold plunges or cold showers your immune system becomes

more active. You don't know about cryotherapy? It's very cool. Haha! So important now with pandemics and so forth. Since the outbreak in the States I've been doing it twice a day. I wish everyone could do it. It's European and goes all the way back to Roman times. They'd take a really hot soak and then do a cold plunge.

They also put lead in their wine! (We laugh.)

What temperature is your cold plunge pool?
I keep mine at 50 degrees, but I'm aiming for 45. It's so invigorating at that temperature. If you rapidly cool the body down, your blood circulation is amplified, the pores snap shut and you get a detoxification.

Interesting! In Chinese medicine we open the pores to detox! How do your joints feel when you do the plunge?
My joint pain completely disappears. It's so amazing. Your joints become totally numb. Completely numb. Even the nerves go numb. No pain! No pain at all. The inflammation disappears. Even muscle spasms disappear. Sports people, health clubs, they're all doing it, they're all reporting it's great for pain. It's like magic.

And how do you feel afterward?
That's the best part—the endorphin rush. You feel invincible, almost ecstatic. And then there are cytokines; tons of them are released. They help you fend off bacteria

and viruses. We need community cold plunge facilities to beat disease. It's really the answer.

How long have you have your plunge pool?
Since we moved in to our house about a year before we got married.

Seven years.
Yes.

Okay, thanks. It very often happens that people come in with serious health issues and we find that they're doing something that is out of alignment with the ancient wisdom of Chinese Medicine. I'm not asking you to change anything, but if you're open to it, I'd like to explain some of this ancient theory that has sustained a massive population for millennia; they must be doing something right! Then you can take it if it makes sense and seems compelling, or leave it if it doesn't, and then we'll do the treatment which will feature moxa on your low back. Moxa is a stick of compressed mugwort or carbon that burns slowly. Holding is carefully and close to certain acupuncture points helps to break up or as we say, scatter cold. You'll feel much better.
Sounds good, I'm all ears.

Firstly, you wouldn't plunge a baby into cold water. And you wouldn't plunge an elderly person into cold water. Do you agree?
Sure, that would be shocking.

Right, and shock is the key word here. You can tell your mind that it will feel a shock and you can tell your mind to tell your body that it will feel a shock and that it will feel great afterward. But the body will still react as if in shock. According to Chinese medicine, the number one cause of all disease is Cold. We even write it with a capital C because it's so important. So a shock involving Cold is a serious shock. One of the most important books in Chinese medical theory is the Shang Han Lun "The Treatise on Diseases Caused By Cold." Seventy percent of that book is about the damage that is caused in the cascade of bodily responses following initial exposure to Cold. This understanding still resonates in Chinese culture. When you go to Chinatown even today, the elderly people are wearing scarves even when it's mild. And you can't buy salads or juices in the standard restaurants.

What about the bubble tea places? Plenty of ice there!

That's just the last couple of decades. In China, away from the tourist areas, you see no salads, no ice, nothing served cold. Even the breakfasts are all warm or hot, or soupy and hot. The people are well covered, especially around the neck where the body is most vulnerable to cold. Hot cooked food is served everywhere all year round even in hot weather. They understand that warmth is essential to longevity and that Cold is the number one enemy.

In Chinese medicine it goes like this: You encounter a cold and the body identifies it as an agent of change. It makes the change and then embarks on eradicating the cold, together with whatever is no longer needed. The first thing it does is activate what we call Kidney Yang. The closest term to this in Western parlance is the word "adrenalin". So you release a little adrenalin which fires up the immune system. (We call the immune system Wei-defensive Qi). The immune system is half adrenaline and half activated fluids. The kidney yang (adrenaline) and stomach yin (fluids) combine forces in the creation of a sneeze and a small sweat, and the pathogenic factor exits. If you have the energy to produce adrenaline, and also a store of adequate expendable fluids, you're free of that pathogen in short shrift.

If that pathogenic factor is not cleared, it penetrates more deeply into the body, and the immune system calls upon more kidney yang to create a fever to try to burn it up. Fever reins until the pathogenic factor is burned up and healing is ensured.

If the body can't generate a fever, or if the fever lingers for long because it can't get high enough, creating dangerous inflammation, an apparent bacterial infection emerges. This is a result of the fever simply not conquering the viral infection. The pathogenic factor proceeds further into the interior. At this point the urgent matter is to keep that factor away from the organs, the viscera, because if the viscera are affected, the situation is potentially deadly: pleuritis, colitis, pancreatitis, gastritis, myocarditis, cystitis, pyelonephritis, hepatitis, cholecystitis, and so on. So the body activates what we call the Divergent Channels. These marvelous Channels have an ingenious mechanism: they gather the pathology and deposit it into the joints. The joints are dense and quiet, a center of synovial fluid that is relatively still. The Divergent Channels dump the cold and the remnants of the body's failed response into the joints where it all becomes latent (hidden away, so that the body can continue to function—to gather food and water, make shelter, and feed the young). In the joints, the pathology waits patiently for the person to regain the resources needed to generate enough warmth to push the pathogen back out into exterior. It waits until has the resources to release the pathogenic factor using a fever and sweat—things it couldn't generate before.

Your Divergent Channels did all that soon after you got your cold plunge pool. Your body was shocked over and over again by the Cold and your body dutifully socked it away. But your joints filled up with the Cold. Then they overflowed. The joints couldn't keep the Cold latent any more. Every time you take a cold plunge now, there's a little bit more Cold to put away but your joints can't capture it. Now it's leaking out into the actual joint structure. Wei-defensive Qi will never give-up trying to redeem the body. It will still go after the Cold even after it has leaked out and penetrated the actual joint structure. But because the pathogen (Cold) has fused with the joint now, the Wei Qi will attack the Cold+Joint combo, thus destroying the bone belonging to the body it is protecting. This is the mechanism of autoimmune diseases.

So why do I feel so amazing after a plunge then. What about the cytokines and the endorphins?

Two things have to feel great for the survival of the human race: sex is one and escaping from danger is another. We're not engineered to run, but when we run fast, we can get a runner's "high". It feels amazing to get away from danger. So when you freeze your body, it thinks it's going to die—which of course it would if you stayed there like Leonardo DiCaprio at the end of Titanic—so you get the adrenaline rush which activates the immune system, releases all those endorphins and cytokines, and then off you go! You feel as though you could solve anything, you feel as though you can get through anything the day has in store for you. You feel invincible. When they take a reading of the blood at that time, your immune system results are staggering: wow! look at the immune system of this guy! Endorphins and cytokines out the roof! Inflammation markers are GONE! Incredible! And it's as hollow, as empty, and as dangerous as 200 foot deep Antarctic crevasse with a layer of snow over it.

But I have so many friends who swear by cold plunges and they don't have arthritis!

They're able to hold the Cold latent longer. They're likely not linking the symptoms to the Cold. And didn't you say that joint pain disappears with the plunge? People couldn't report that unless they had joint pain in the first place. They're going around in circles, perhaps.

So how would you get your endorphins to release?

You can get a release of cytokines and endorphins by meditating, by brisk walking, by loving someone, by admiring a tree. But our culture is looking for thrills. We've become so numbed to dumb culture, the celebration of meaningless inconsequential things, to the mindless parts of social media, to violence on the screen, to vapid video games. These things can't compete with the way endorphins are released in meditation, in loving, in walking in nature. We don't need endorphin and cytokine rushes, we need a steady gentle background hum of them. And you told me your wife is a dream and you love your job. Do you need this shocking of your body to give you these expensive thrills?
Expensive?

Yes, it's extremely expensive. The capacity to produce kidney yang (adrenaline) is finite. You're born with a certain amount in your life-force bank account. You can replenish it to a certain degree but only with warm, hot and cooked foods, and going early to bed. The bottom line is that it runs out, and when it does, death arrives. The more you force your adrenal glands into action, the less time you have.
Are you saying that my cold plunges are actually reducing my capacity to fight off illness?

Yes. Every time you call on kidney yang or adrenaline by eliciting urgent sudden responses from the body, you are a little less able to create the next immune response. Then you'll crank up the ante. You'll turn your plunge pool temperature down a little, you'll get confrontational, you'll take a risk in business or while driving your car that you shouldn't have taken, and that will stimulate a bigger response which will make you feel more alive again. The end of that pattern is early death. I've seen people do this with heat, too. They'll tell me they want to take extremely hot baths and that they wish they could tolerate hotter and hotter water. They, too, are trying to stimulate kidney yang, and it will respond because remember kidney yang finances the immune system which makes you sweat, either to expel something if you have a cold, or to cool you off if you're overheated. That's still kidney yang. The end of that pattern is also its expenditure, leading to early death, or a lifetime of disease.

But what about living life. Just getting out of bed takes energy!

Yes, all action takes a little kidney yang. Getting out of bed for most is the first step in the day of living life. We live our lives and when our resources (kidney yang) is all used up, we exit our worn out bodies.

Kidney yang and its balancing (yin) partner, are precious jewels. You can't even find them in the pulses of a healthy person until you dig down deep in the pulse where they sit quietly in a luscious wide band. The response to every shock, every rejection, every adverse reaction, every argument, every fight, every emergency, every assault on the body steals these most precious commodities away. They are not to be disturbed too much. To live calmly, to live peacefully, to live lovingly, to be happy in our work, to allow our contributions to drive us steadily, calmly and without fear—this is how we preserve our very life force.

Now, it's time for moxa. We'll begin the process of breaking up this systemic cold to free your joints of their cold burden. You'll feel so much better with some Heat!

Sounds great. Can we close the window, by the way?

Yes, of course, I can even heat the table if you'd like that.

Spectacular!

A Note to Acupuncturists and Channel Practitioners:

We'd spent most of the hour in discussion about Cold. If a patient is not educated in the mechanism of their illness, the treatment is thrown away when they re-engage in the very thing that's making them ill. The teaching must be done without pointing the finger (without directing the teaching to the patient personally), without blame or judgment, and without superiority. It's simply delivered as a teaching.

I applied moxa on GV-4 for quite a while, then KI-2 and SP-8 and then CV-12 to get the Spleen into gear so that he could begin manufacturing Wei Qi again. We'll see how the pulses look next week; hopefully they will be relaxed enough to reveal which medium is lacking most. Clearly the Divergents are called for but not yet. We need to break up some of the cold first. Trying to pull the Cold using the Divergents now would lead to a partial clearing since there may be insufficient media to carry it out. That would lead to an autointoxication as the pathology is partially released. The pain would increase. Next week, when I can read the various commodities in the pulses, I'll know which Divergent to treat and it will be deep-superficial-deep technique, to more completely contain the pathogen and keep it quiet as we shore up the body's resources to create the healing it's unable to perform. The correct Divergent could be any of them, even the Lung Divergent. Divergent Channels treat pathology that is affecting the structure. The Divergent Channel chosen will contain the pathology so that the joint pain is alleviated, and ultimately the channel will facilitate the exit of the Cold. When the exit occurs, it could look like a flu, so that will be part of our next conversation.

Update: Three months after the first encounter the patient is clear of joint pain, not simply due to acupuncture and moxa, but because the patient stopped the plunges and only eats cooked warm food. He reports the change as feeling like a miracle, but of course it is not, it's just classical Chinese medicine in action.

Ann
Manhattan, 2020.

Appendix 3
Organ functions

Note that when Chinese medicine practitioners talks about organ function, they are referring not just to the organ, but mainly to the channel of energy that flows from the arms or legs and then through that organ. The channel adds what we call "qi directionality," adding many dimensions as it carries out the function of each organ.

The Lungs and their channel manage energy, move qi down, and move qi out to the exterior of the body. The lungs move blood and fluids to moisten the body, and they allow a person to let go of emotions, to forgive, and to accept.

The Heart is the home of the spirit and elicits the sharing of love and joy. Its channel connects to the tongue to enable openhearted speech and to the eyes where its light can be seen. The heart governs circulation of blood including the movement of blood to the periphery.

The Spleen and Pancreas and their channel govern digestion, the extraction and transport of nutrients from food, and the production of qi. This organ system is responsible for the health of the musculature, the arms and legs, and the postural integrity of the body, including the internal organs. The spleen is responsible for upward movement: holding things up, moving blood up to the heart, moving qi up to the digestive tract, moving fluids up to the sensory orifices, and moving qi up to the lungs. It also manages and discharges swellings and accumulations. The spleen manages blood, governing its manufacture and keeping it from leaking. It also manages thoughts and the mind.

The Liver and its channel regulates and courses qi, ensuring its smooth flow. The liver has the capacity to discharge inflamed swellings (damp-heat) through the bladder. It stores blood and provides the foundational qi and blood for creativity, self-esteem, and the heart and kidneys. It brings blood to the musculature, brain, eyes, hair roots, nails, and reproductive system. As the gate to the collective unconscious, its qi enables one to plan and to remember.

The Kidneys and their channel control reproduction, growth, decay, decline, and the lower orifices. They maintain bones, structure, shape, form, and regulate the passage of water. The kidneys house the will and determination to follow one's path. They secure the constitution, receive qi from the breath, and generate the distribution of our moving and warming yang qi.

Acknowledgments

Thank you Cody Dodo for yet another book beautifully designed.

Thank you Ravi Zohar Sterman for your exquisite photographs.

Thank you Andrew Sterman, Mark Phillips, Jordan Lo Piccolo, Neil and Marika Bender, Mónica Martin Prats, Miriam Sterman, Susan Proctor, Dorian Hastings, Kathleen Furlong, Gabrielle Zlotnik, Holly Peppe, Dar Dowling, Susan Plourde, Chelsea Horenstein, Gretchen Krieger, Linda Puckette, Tim Turco, Hung Tran, Doug McGill, Peter McCraw, Setareh Moafi and Salvador Cefalu. Thank you Ariel Daunay for your deep care of our family.
Thank you to all my patients and students who have proven beyond any doubt how much is truly possible.

Thank you Master Jeffrey Yuen to whom I remain lovingly grateful.

About the Author

Ann Cecil-Sterman is the author of the widely acclaimed books: *The Art of Pulse Diagnosis*, *Illustrations of the Complete Acupuncture System*, *Tongue Diagnosis*, and *Advanced Acupuncture: A Clinic Manual*, a required text in many acupuncture schools. Currently she teaches a six month training and mentorship immersion program to students on five continents every year. She also travels extensively to reach students in person for refining practice of the Complement Channels, pulse diagnosis, and with her husband, Andrew Sterman, the use of food as medicine. For many years she taught Advanced Clinical Observation and was a senior clinic supervisor at the school of acupuncture in New York founded in 1997 by the great master Jeffrey Yuen, who was her teacher for over twenty years. Her patients—children and adults of all ages—have come from all over the world to work through illnesses or on personal cultivation. She lives in Manhattan with her family. www.anncecilsterman.com

About the Photographer

Ravi Zohar Sterman is a photographer and artist. He studied at the Pratt Institute in New York. His photographs have appeared at the Metropolitan Museum of Art and in various magazines.

About the Designer

Cody Dodo studied acupuncture under Master Jeffrey Yuen at the Swedish Institute in New York and later completed advanced studies with him in acupuncture and Chinese dietary therapy. Prior to his pursuit of acupuncture, Cody had a long career as a graphic designer in the publishing industry. Cody teaches Classical Acupuncture internationally, and is dedicated to the transmission of this wonderful medicine. He also designed the author's other books, *Advanced Acupuncture: A Clinic Manual*, *Illustrations of the Complete Acupuncture System*, *The Art of Pulse Diagnosis* and *Tongue Diagnosis*.

By the Same Author

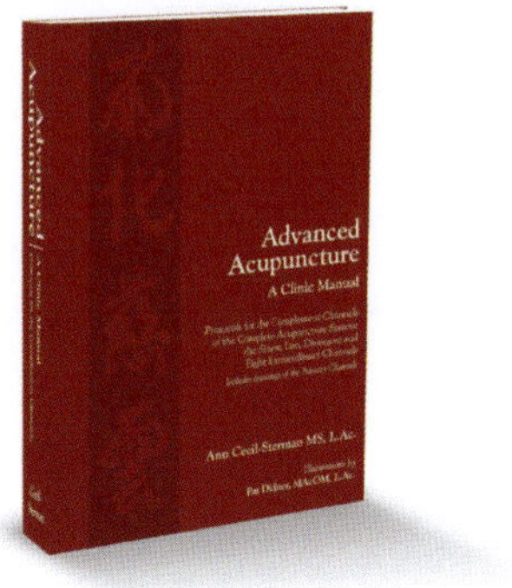

Advanced Acupuncture, A Clinic Manual

Protocols for the Complement Channels of the Complete Acupuncture System: the Sinew, Luo, Divergent and Eight Extraordinary Channels.

Classical Wellness Press, 2012, 2018 (2nd Ed)

Currently a required or recommended text in many acupuncture schools.

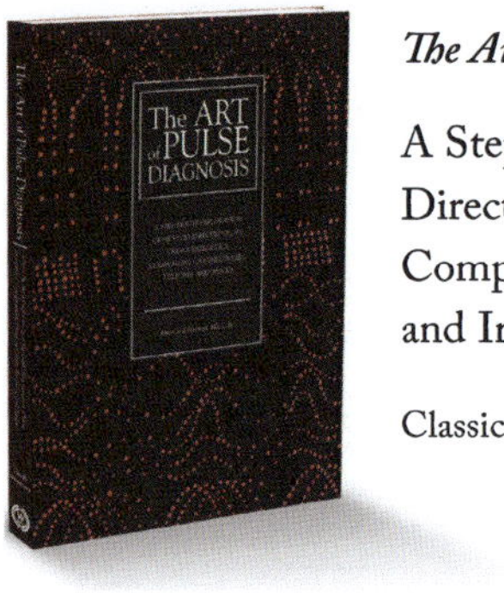

The Art of Pulse Diagnosis

A Step-by-Step Exploration of Method, Directionality, Organ Energetics, Complement Channel Pulses, Textures and Images.

Classical Wellness Press, 2015

Illustrations of the Complete Acupuncture System: the Sinew, Luo, Divergent, Eight Extraordinary and Primary Channels

Classical Wellness Press, 2014

(This is a companion volume to *Advanced Acupuncture, A Clinic Manual.*)

And introducing...

Welcoming Food: Diet as Medicine for Home Cooks and Other Healers

2 volumes

by Andrew Sterman

Classical Wellness Press, 2020

Printed in Great Britain
by Amazon

25180382R00087